HOW TO DRAW IN
PASTELS PENCILS AND PEN & INK

CONTENTS

Pastel

WHILE PASTELS are generally considered a drawing medium, working with them involves both painting and drawing skills. The same principles apply to pastels as to many painting media as seen in the overlaying of colors to create new colors and transparency.

The main difference between using pastel and the usual painting media is that the former cannot be easily erased or corrected. The artist's only recourse to correcting a pastel drawing is to overlay more color. For this reason the picture should be developed through careful and well thought-out layering of tone and color rather than through heavy and dense application of the pastels.

In this picture the artist has used some elements of the pointillist technique without the use of 'points'. Rather, thin strokes of pure color have been laid down beside and on top of one another to give the impression of mixing colors and tones. The picture is based primarily on the use of warm and cool colors – red and blue – and their interaction with one another. By careful use of complementary colors, such as a touch of a reddish tone in a predominantly blue area, a dull and predictable picture is avoided. Close examination of the finished picture reveals that where there is a large area of one color – blue for example – its complement, red, has been added to give the picture unity. The complementary color also 'bounces off' the other warm color areas, unifying the picture as a whole.

Materials

Surface
Heavy weight pastel paper

Size
18.5in × 26in (46cm × 65cm)

Tools
Willow charcoal
Rags or tissues
Fixative

Colors
Blue-green	Light red
Cobalt blue	Light yellow
Crimson	Orange
Dark blue	Pale blue
Dark green	Yellow

1. With broad strokes, lay in the basic warm and cool colors as an underpainting.

2. With heavier, linear strokes, begin to develop darker tones of these general color areas moving over the paper with one color at a time.

3. Begin to lay in lighter, warmer tones of orange, yellow, and red building up the color contrasts of the warm-cool, blue-red motif. Keep the strokes light.

4. Return to the dark colors previously used, heightening shadow areas with a heavier stroke.

5. With cobalt blue, lighten any areas which appear too heavy or dark. Put in the sky with pale blue.

6. Return to the dark blue, red, and green colors to put in the final touches of emphasis and contrast using stroke to give direction and shape.

Overlaying pure color

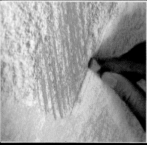

With pastel, the artist produces colors which mix optically on the surface by applying thin lines of pure color one over the other. Here, pale blue strokes are laid over crimson in the wall to create an impression of purple.

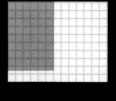

WORKING WITH OIL pastels requires a slightly different approach and attitude than using the traditional chalk type of pastel. Unlike chalk pastels, oil pastels can be used as a painting medium. They can be softened and mixed on a palette and then directly applied to the surface with a palette knife; or thinned with turpentine and then wiped onto the surface with a rag. Pastels of any type are difficult to correct, and oil pastels more difficult than most. Without the aid of turpentine, a rag, and some heavy rubbing, the strokes you put down are permanent. For this reason, use a fairly light touch in the preliminary stages of the drawing.

In this painting, the artist has used a variety of techniques to exploit the medium's potential to its fullest and has literally painted with the pastels using all the techniques normally ascribed to traditional oil painting.

Due to their rich and thick texture, another effective technique is to scratch back through the pastel to reveal the original surface color. This can be achieved with any sharp tool to create a variety of lines and tones from a dense crosshatching to a light and flowing line.

Materials

Surface
Stretched, strong cartridge paper

Size
9in × 7in (22cm × 17.5cm)

Tools
2B pencil
Palette knife
Q-tips
Rags or tissues
Pen knife

Oil pastel colors
Black	Ultramarine blue
Cerulean blue	White
Payne's grey	

Medium
Turpentine

1. Make a preliminary sketch in pencil of the main features and compositional structure of the picture.

2. At this point, do not worry about the details of the picture, but loosely rough in the basic sea, sky, and land colors with loose, diagonal strokes.

3. Cover this layer with a thick, opaque white and shades of grey. Blend with a palette knife, pressing hard into the surface. Scratch back with edge of knife.

4. Over this, lay in the dark areas of the sky and horizon with ultramarine blue. Create foreground waves with white applied in short strokes.

Using the palette knife · blending

5. Dip a Q-tip in turpentine and blend the pastel over the entire picture surface to cover any remaining white areas.

6. Put a darker grey in the sky, using diagonal strokes. Lay in light areas of waves and land with white, or scratch back to white of surface with a knife.

7. Heighten the contrast in the foreground waves by adding more directional strokes of dark grey.

Here the artist is seen pressing small pieces of oil pastel onto the surface with a broad palette knife. The knife, like a brush, can be used to create directional strokes and textures.

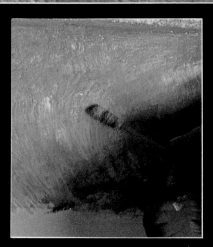

With a Q-tip dipped in turpentine, the artist works over the oil pastel surface, blending colours and covering white gaps in the surface.

8. Add deeper blue touches around the white of the wave crests to heighten this contrast.

Pencil

COLORED PENCILS have a special relevance to landscape drawing, especially when the artist wishes to depict the effects of sun and shadow. The variety of lights and darks which can be achieved with colored pencils allows the artist to either work with a very pale and delicate range of colors and tone, or with a very intense and bold palette. When the two are combined – a pale, loose stroke and an intense and colorful area – the effect is balanced yet dynamic. In this case, the combination of architecture and nature is well suited to the medium, and vice versa.

Much like painting media, colored pencils allow the artist to build up layer upon layer of subtle color to create a transparent effect. For instance, crosshatching in different colors – overlaying one area of colored strokes over another color – can create an interesting tone and texture in the picture.

Drawing with colored pencil requires patience and thoroughness. The point of the pencil being relatively small, it is difficult to cover large areas with any evenness of tone and stroke. A smooth, hardish paper or board is normally used with pencil work, however, a roughly textured surface can create interesting white 'gaps' and grainy effects.

Materials

Surface
Stretched, rough drawing paper

Size
30in × 25in (75cm × 62.5cm)

Tools
Eraser
Pencil sharpener or small knife

Colors
Cerulean blue	Light yellow
Chrome green	Medium yellow
Dark brown	Ultramarine blue
Dark green	Yellow ochre

1. After sketching in general shapes with blue pencil, develop general shadow areas with blue and brown pencils.

3. Put in dark areas with black and dark brown pencils. Crosshatch using different colors and directional strokes to create color and tone.

5. Carry the light yellow and ochre tones into the foreground and palm tree.

7. Put in very loose strokes of brown in the middle distance. With a strong stroke, develop the green of the foreground palm. Highlight very bright areas with white.

2. With a pale yellow pencil, begin to put in the lighter areas of the wooden structure. This 'underpainting' will ensure a feeling of bright daylight.

4. Work from the centre outward to maintain the picture's focal point. Build up shapes using ultramarine blue for the darker areas.

6. Build up a strong, detailed drawing of the foreground palm with pale and dark green tones.

8. Carry loose, blue strokes over the foreground to indicate shadow.

Palm textures · overlaying dark colors · developing shadows

Working around the shape of the far dome, the artist overlays a dark green area with light green strokes.

In the initial steps, the artist begins to block in areas of dark color as in the windows of the house.

To create the texture of a palm tree, the artist overlays thin strokes of color.

BECAUSE PAINTING equipment is often difficult and cumbersome to manage out of doors, many landscape artists prefer to do rough sketches which are later used as reference for paintings. However, many landscape drawings are interesting as pictures in their own right.

The drawing shown has many qualities both in terms of pencil technique and subject which are worth noting. Notice that the artist has chosen a strong vertical space in which to draw. This is not typical of most landscape work which is generally done in the 'landscape', or horizontal position. The picture itself, however, is described using horizontal strokes which serves to create an interesting contrast between the shape of the overall image and the image itself.

A putty eraser is very effective in creating highlights. After the general tones have been laid down, the artist can work into the picture erasing out light or highlight areas. These can later be modified by working over again in pencil, or strengthened by further erasing.

Materials

Surface
Cartridge paper

Size
6in × 18in (15cm × 45cm)

Tools
2B, 4B pencils
Putty eraser
Fixative

1. With a 2B pencil, sketch in the perimeter of the drawing and very lightly block in the sky and land shapes.

2. With a 4B pencil, block in the foreground tone and work into darker areas. Keep the strokes loose and light.

3. Work back into the clouds with the same pencil developing a stronger tone.

4. Using the tip of a putty eraser, work over cloud shapes using the same directional strokes as used with the pencil.

Erasing

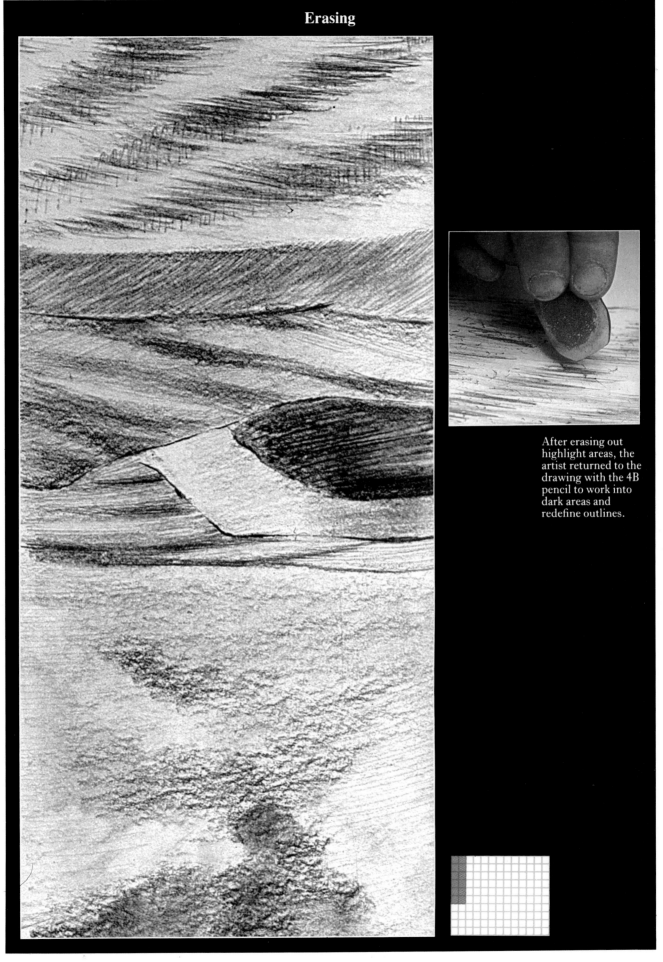

After erasing out highlight areas, the artist returned to the drawing with the 4B pencil to work into dark areas and redefine outlines.

DRAWING IS IN many ways similar to sculpture. The sculptor, while carving out a shape, is always concerned with the space around the shape – the 'holes' which the observer will see through. This is known as negative space; a concept often difficult to grasp but essential to the success of a drawing or painting, especially when the artist wishes to exploit the use of 'white space' or the blank paper.

The drawing shown here is an excellent example of the use of negative and white space. While the artist used the pencils to create an image, he has also used the white of the paper to emphasize shapes and areas between and around the forms. An example is the thin line of red placed diagonally behind the plants. The observer reads this as a 'wall'; no more than this simple line is needed to create the impression of space and depth.

The picture also shows that the entire surface need not be covered to create an effective drawing. If you imagine the picture with all the white areas filled in, you would see that the drawing would lose much of its graphic impact. It takes practice to know when to stop a drawing. Very often the impact of a drawing can be lessened or lost if overworked or carried too far.

Materials

Surface
Smooth, heavy weight drawing paper

Size
23.5in × 17in (59cm × 42cm)

Tools
B, 2B, 4B drawing pencils
Eraser
Ruler

Colors
Black	Dark green
Blue-green	Light green
Dark grey	Red

1. Very lightly sketch in a small area of the subject with a 2B pencil and begin to define leaf shapes and background with dark green and black, pressing firmly.

2. Using a diagonal stroke, carry the dark green color on to the next area, lightly hatching in the area and then reworking. Put in red line with ruler.

3. Continue to work around this small area, defining the palm leaves in tones of grey and green, first working lightly and then building up heavier, detail areas.

4. Work back into previous areas with black and green pencils, strengthening the darks with a heavy, dense stroke.

5. With blue-green and dark green, begin to put in the cactus shape.

Finished picture · underdrawing

In order to successfully balance the composition of the drawing, in the last step the artist described the palm tree on the far right. Note that only pale colors and a light touch were used; the tree serves to balance the picture but does not overwhelm the left hand side.

With a light blue pencil, the artist is here putting in the first layer of color which will later be developed by overlaying different colors.

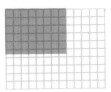

Pen and ink

PEN AND INK has a long tradition in both landscape and architectural drawing. It is especially well suited for the latter as a variety of lines and textures can be created without losing the linear qualities inherent in a city-scape. It is a good medium for working out of doors as well. With pen, pad, and bottle of ink, the artist can situate himself anywhere for either quick sketching or detailed drawing.

Ink is a very flexible medium and can be used in a variety of ways. The usual technique is to use only the pen, nib, and ink; this in itself will provide you with an unlimited choice in terms of line and tone. In this instance, the artist has chosen the traditional use of line for the initial sketch only and has proceeded to develop the picture through the use of innovative and unconventional tools. A thumb can be used to create unusual shadows and textures; the side of a box, when dipped in ink and pressed on to the surface gives an intriguing 'architectural' effect. Spattering the ink with a toothbrush will create a fine mist similar to an aquatint.

If working out of doors there may be many interesting objects around you which can be used in a similar fashion – drawing with a stick, 'printing' with a leaf, dipping some grass in ink and drawing it across the page.

Materials

Surface
Smooth, white cartridge paper

Size
16.5in × 12in (41cm × 30cm)

Tools
Pen holder	Toothbrush
Fine and medium nibs	Small knife
Masking tape	Small box

Colors
Black waterproof India ink

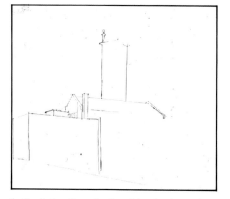

1. Begin by directly sketching in the main verticals and horizontals of the picture with a fine nib.

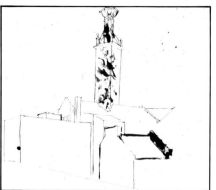

2. Use the back of the pen to create a thick, emphatic line. The thumb can be used to develop an interesting shadow texture as in the tower.

Finished picture · blotting with finger · spattering

In the last step, the artist put in very faint cloud shapes. This was accomplished by tearing pieces of paper and using their rough edges as a mask over which a fine mist of ink was spattered. Very light lines were then put in to define the shapes. Details were then re-emphasized.

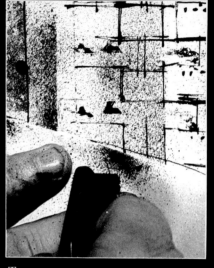

To create a spattered effect, dip a toothbrush in ink and, masking the area not to be spattered with a piece of paper, draw a finger quickly through the brush bristles.

Dipping a finger in ink and blotting it on to the surface creates an interesting texture. In this case, the sharp, crisp lines of the tower work well with the greyish smudges caused by the finger.

3. Use the back of the pen to develop the foreground objects. Dip the end of a small box in ink and press lightly to the surface for a brick-like effect.

4. Build up dark areas by defining geometric shapes and details with a medium nib.

5. Dip a toothbrush in ink and mask the area not to be covered with tape. Run a knife blade quickly over the brush to create spatters.

WHEN USING the traditional pen, nib, and ink it is important to note that it is basically a linear form of rendering. The marks are definite and not easily erased, and 'colors' must be created by hatched and scribbled strokes rather than blending. It is important to understand such characteristics and limitations which will enable you to focus your attention on aspects of the subject which lend themselves to the descriptive qualities of the medium.

When working in pen and ink, look for a subject with a strong, linear emphasis, well-defined motifs and dense pattern or texture. A good range of colored inks is available; there is no need to consider this a primarily monochrome medium. The colors form the intermediary tones between black and the clear white of the paper. Until you feel confident in handling color, however, it may be well to restrict yourself to a few basic tones.

Start by roughing out a simple linear framework for the drawing and then work into each area in detail, gradually building up the overall pattern. Develop a range of marks which correspond to the natural forms and textures without trying to reproduce every shape in detail. As the work progresses, adjust the density of the colors and patterns to achieve a satisfactory tonal balance.

Materials

Surface
White cartridge paper

Size
18.5in × 26in (46cm × 65cm)

Tools
Thick, square-nibbed pen
Fine mapping pen

Colors
April green   Deep green
Black   Sunshine yellow

1. Draw up the general outline of the image in black ink using a large, broad-nibbed pen. Indicate the main elements with fluid, linear strokes.

3. Build up a textured surface to suggest the grass with scratchy, criss-crossed marks, overlaying green and black.

5. Contrast the strong black textures with a thin layer of green crosshatching in the background. Draw with a fine pen using quick, light strokes.

2. Work over the whole image again in black starting to define the shapes and forms in detail, using thick and thin nibs.

4. Draw into the large tree in black, making heavy shadows with broad pen strokes. Work over the black with green and yellow.

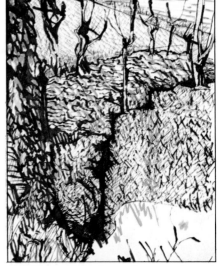

6. Fill in the central area of grass and leaves with a woven pattern of green and black marks. Draw together the separate sections of the image.

Outlining

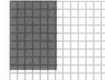

With a broad-nibbed pen, the artist is here putting in the general outlines of the picture. The width of the line is varied by turning the pen while drawing.

FINE, LINEAR DRAWING with pen and ink requires a careful, deliberate approach. Tonal shading must be developed gradually and crosshatching cannot be rapidly blocked in. The crisp, emphatic lines of a pen drawing have no equivalent and it is worthwhile to acquire the skill and patience to handle the pen to produce the dramatic, graphic effects of this medium.

This drawing gives a general impression of a landscape by starting with a loose sketch which outlines shapes and positions of trees and bushes. Each area of hatched lines and irregular, scribbled marks correspond to the basic tonal and textural structure. While the elements are treated separately, the whole image is constantly considered as a whole and brought together in the final stages.

Your technique should be controlled but not rigid – keep the pen well charged with ink and make decisive, fluid strokes. Even if the drawing is quite small, the marks should be as vigorous as possible, since it is texture, not color, which provides visual interest. Keep a lively balance in the tones by working some areas more densely than others and by varying the direction of the strokes and character of the marks.

Materials

Surface
Thick white cartridge paper

Size
12in × 8in (30cm × 20cm)

Tools
HB pencil
Dip pen
Medium nib

Colors
Black waterproof India ink

1. Make a light sketch of the layout with an HB pencil. Start to draw with the pen showing rough outlines and tones.

2. Develop the tones using the large tree as a focal point and working outwards. Build up the texture with fluid scribbled marks and crisp lines.

Crosshatching tones

3. Work across the paper sketching in shapes and elaborating forms.

4. Extend the hatched tones, establishing receding planes and overall shape of the image. Develop details in the foreground with small, irregular patterns.

5. Concentrate on details, particularly in the foreground, and work over the outlines of the shapes to soften the contours.

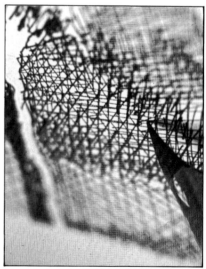

This detail of the shadow area behind the tree shows the artist using crosshatching to develop dense and varied tonal areas.

Pastel

IN TERMS OF color, shape, and gesture, the subject for this picture is well suited to a pastel drawing as bold colors and sharp, gestural strokes are few of the many potential uses of pastel. Of course the technique used will determine the end result; if this picture had been executed with heavy blending, smudging and subtle color the results would be quite different.

The colors used are basically complementary: red, orange and pink; blue, purple and green. It is worth remembering that color is created by light, and color will always reflect and bounce off neighboring colors. The artist has exploited this by using a complementary color within a predominant color area. Thus there are touches of red in the purple flowers, and touches of purple in the red and orange flowers. The dark blue used to describe the stems and shadow areas works as a contrast to both the purple, blue, and red, intensifying and adding depth to the overall picture.

The composition was purposely arranged to give a feeling of closeness. The white of the paper works in stark contrast to the densely clustered stems and flowers in the bottom left corner and the directional strokes serve to lead the eye upward and across the page.

Materials

Surface
Pastel paper

Size
16in × 20in (40cm × 50cm)

Tools
Tissue or rag
Willow charcoal
Fixative

Colors
Blue-green	Orange
Cadmium red medium	Pale blue
Cadmium yellow medium	Pink
Cobalt blue	Prussian blue
Dark green	White
Light green	

1. After roughing in the flower shapes with charcoal, lightly sketch in the flowers in pink, red, and purple and the stems in light and dark greens.

2. With a small piece of tissue, blend the color tones of the flowers. With pale blue, work back into the purple flowers describing the petals with sharp strokes.

A method of blending is to use a small piece of tissue. Unlike a finger, the tissue will both blend colors and pick up the pastel, thus lightening the tone.

Pastel marks can either be left as clean strokes or blended into subtle gradations of tone and color. Here the artist is blending within the flowers, mixing the orange and pink.

Using the tip of a pastel, the artist describes stem and leaf shapes with a quick, loose motion.

3. With cadmium red and orange, emphasize the petal shapes with sharp strokes. With dark blue, define stems with the same sharp, directional strokes.

4. With purple pastel, put a heavier layer down within the blue flowers. Use the same color to put in additional leaf and stem shapes with a loose stroke.

5. Returning to the flowers, apply deeper tones with more pressure. Add touches of red to the purple flowers. Create flower centers with yellow in the pink flowers.

Finished picture blending · stem and leaf shapes

To finish the picture (<u>right</u>), the artist continued to develop strong dark areas with blue. As a final step, a tissue was used to pick up loose color and blend into the right hand corner.

PERFECTING THE techniques needed to draw effectively in pastel takes time. As pastels are loose and powdery, the sticks must be carefully manipulated to achieve any degree of precision. If you work on tinted paper, the light tones may be handled as positive, strong colors while the tint adds depth to the overall tone of the work.

Outlines, where used, should be light and sketchy, merely providing a guideline to be eventually overlaid by areas of color. Spray the drawing with fixative whenever necessary to keep the colors bright and stable. Overlay layers of color with light strokes of the pastels to create soft, intermediary tones.

Materials

Surface
Blue pastel paper

Size
11in × 15in (27cm × 37cm)

Tools
Fixative

Colors

Black	Orange
Cobalt blue	Pink
Dark and light green	White
Dark and light red	Yellow

1. Loosely sketch in the basic position of the bird with red and orange pastels. Draw the crest of the head in white.

3. Construct a solid impression of shape, drawing into the form with white and black. Work into the background with light tones.

5. Strengthen the colour over the whole image, showing shadows and highlights. Overlay scribbled patches of different colors.

2. Work over the drawing with vigorous, scribbled marks, contrasting the orange and red of the bird against green and yellow in the background.

4. Strengthen outlines on the bird in black and lay in a dark green behind. Add small details in blue and white.

6. Spray the drawing with fixative and let it dry. Reinforce the red shapes, giving the form more definition. Work up linear details in the background.

Developing general shapes and tones · highlighting

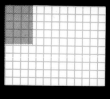

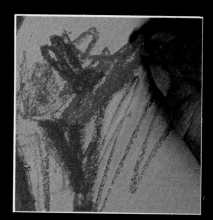

Here the artist begins to block in the color of the bird with a very loose, scribbling motion.

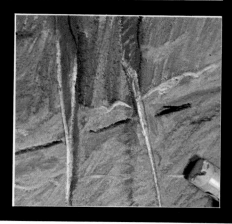

With pale yellow, the artist moves across the picture putting in loose lines of highlight.

Pencil

WASH AND LINE illustrates the ability of mixed media to capture an image both simply and directly. By a skillfull use of line and carefully placed touches of wash, the artist is able to reduce the subject to its bare essentials, creating a picture which is fresh and simple in style.

How to decide upon the ratio of line to wash, and vice versa, takes practice and a keen eye. There are no hard and fast rules but, in general, it is best to keep the image as clear and uncluttered as possible. The temptation to cover the surface with many colors and techniques is a common one; it takes practice, restraint, and a critical eye to put into the picture only what is absolutely essential to best express the subject.

A good reason for resisting the temptation to cover the page is that often the plain white surface can emphasize a line or dab of color far more than any techniques or additional colors can. It is the use of contrast – the broad white or tinted paper contrasting with the sharp edge of a line or subtle wash of color – which serves to emphasize and draw attention to the image. The emptiness and cleanness of a few well-chosen lines and dots of color, when combined with the untouched surface can create an image of eye-catching simplicity.

Materials

Surface
Thick cartridge paper

Size
26in × 18in (65cm × 45cm)

Tools
4B pencil
Putty eraser

Colors
Gold ochre watercolor

Medium
Water

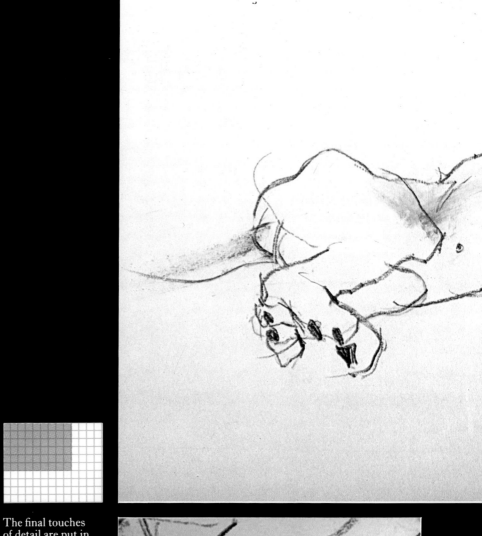

The final touches of detail are put in with a soft, dark pencil.

1. Begin by putting a small amount of gold ochre directly on to a small piece of rag.

2. Rub the gold ochre on to the surface to create general color areas. Use your finger or fingers to draw with the paint and create feathered textures similar to fur.

Feathering · drawing in shapes · details

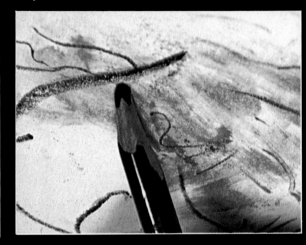

With a dense
stroke, the artist is
here seen working
over the yellow wash
to put in the general
shape of the lion.

A feathered
texture can be
achieved by using
the fingers to lightly
touch the paint on to
the surface. Do not
use too much paint
on the rag and do
not dilute with
turpentine.

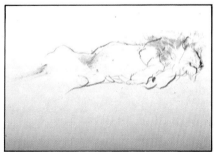

3. With a soft, dark pencil, begin to
describe the lion's head over the gold ochre
paint. Vary the thickness and width of the
line.

4. With the same pencil, continue down
the body of the lion with a light, flowing
stroke.

5. Reinforce outlines with more pressure.
Put in dark details in the head and feet.

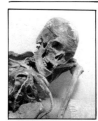

A SKULL is a good subject for a pencil drawing as it has a fluid and well-defined outline. The overall structure however is quite complex, containing a variety of linear and tonal details. The smooth, rounded dome of the skull demands subtle changes of tone which contrast with the dense, black shadows in the sockets of the eyes, nose and mouth.

The forms are represented by overlaid layers of shading and crosshatching married with crisp lines outlining the shapes and describing small fissures in the surface. Allow the image to emerge gradually by first developing the structure as a broad view of the whole shape and then breaking down each area to show details.

Arrange the subject carefully when you start a drawing to make sure it presents an interesting view which shows clearly the qualities to be described by the drawing medium. Use an HB pencil in the early stages moving on to a softer 2B to reinforce the lines and dark tones. If you work slowly and logically over the form it may not be necessary to use an eraser, but be prepared to make continual minor adjustments as the drawing develops. Vary the direction of the hatched lines to correspond to the network of curves and cavities. In this case, other bones have been drawn in to establish a horizontal plane and so the shape is not isolated.

Materials

Surface
Thick cartridge paper

Size
18in × 20in (45cm × 50cm)

Tools
HB and 2B pencils
Putty eraser
Fixative

1. Use an HB pencil to sketch in the outline of the skull and the sockets of the eyes and nose. Work loosely with line and light hatching, strengthening the shape.

2. Extend the outline shape and start to hatch in dark shadows, working the pencil in different directions to intensify the tones.

3. Develop the structure with a 2B pencil. Work over the whole drawing blocking in small shapes and improving the definition of the contours.

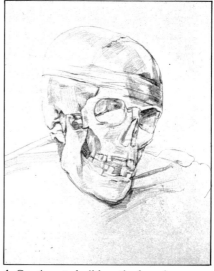

4. Continue to build up the form in more detail, drawing small shapes of the teeth and jaw socket. Use an eraser where necessary to make corrections.

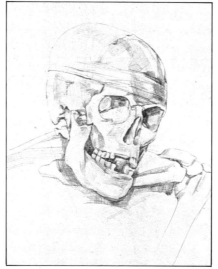

5. Strengthen the outlines and work over dark tones with crosshatched lines to give depth and bring out the full volume of the form.

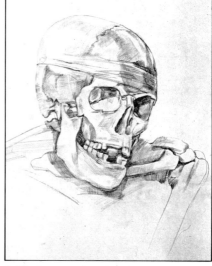

6. Work across the whole image making minor adjustments in the tonal balance and reinforcing the lines where appropriate to clarify the overall structure.

Crosshatching the eye area

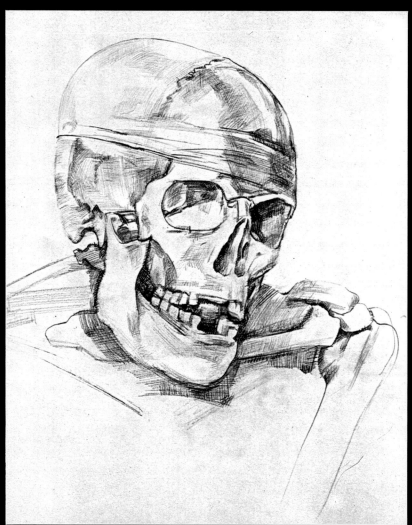

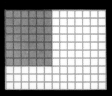

The artist is seen here working into the eye cavity with a soft, dark pencil. Note the use of crosshatching to create depth. The darker the hatching, the more the shape will appear to recede.

Crosshatching the eye area

WILLOW CHARCOAL IS often used for preliminary sketches for paintings but it is also an exciting medium in its own right. The most enjoyable aspect of drawing with willow charcoal is its responsiveness to touch and stroke. Another important feature is that it is easily erased – the artist can put down very intense, black areas and either lighten or remove these entirely with a putty eraser or tissue. The line achieved with willow charcoal is soft and fluid but by no means weak. A wide variety of tones and textures can be achieved through the use of line, tone, blending, and erasing.

The picture here is a good example of the various techniques available. The artist has relied purely on tone, texture, and stroke to give the animal weight and to distinguish it from its surroundings. The elephant is described in soft, blended tones, while the background is created with bold, directional strokes each offsetting the other.

The picture developed through a constant movement between dark and light areas and lines. A dark area is put in, lightened, and then the artist again returned to the dark areas. As seen in the steps, there was a constant progression from light to dark and back again, but within this there was a constant adjustment and readjustment of shadow and highlight, soft and bold, blended areas and linear strokes.

Materials

Surface
Rough drawing paper

Size
23.5in × 22in (59cm × 55cm)

Tools
2B pencil
Medium and light willow charcoal
Putty eraser
Tissues
Fixative

1. After putting in the general shape and composition of the drawing in light pencil, redraw the outline of the animal and background with fine willow charcoal.

2. Using the side of a piece of light charcoal, rough in shadow areas of animal. With a piece of medium charcoal, quickly sketch in the background.

Erasing highlights · laying in tones

In the first few steps, broad areas of tone are laid down using the side of the charcoal.

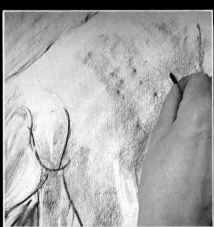

A putty eraser may be used to create highlights. Here the artist is erasing back through the charcoal, blocking in light areas.

3. With medium charcoal, work back into the shadow areas of the elephant in loose strokes. Blend area around eye with finger. With putty eraser, erase highlights.

4. Develop darks in background by putting down strokes and blending. Rework outline of elephant. Blend shadow areas beneath with tissue or finger.

5. With heavy, gestural strokes, put in background. Strengthen darks in elephant and blend. Use putty eraser to clean up whites and highlight areas.

Pen and ink

THE LOOSE LINE and confident strokes which experienced pen and ink artists achieve are acquired more by a relaxed attitude than superior drawing talents. More than any other medium, if the artist is worried about his strokes, the pen and ink drawing will immediately reveal his concern; the artist must make a conscious effort to overcome a desire to control or inhibit the line of the pen and the flow of the ink.

The artist has here achieved an informal sketch with little detail or careful rendering. The strokes are loose, flowing, casual. While there are many artists who consider any form of correction wrong, it is perfectly acceptable to correct a pen and ink drawing, as the artist has done here, with white gouache. On the other hand, as it is impossible to draw over lumps of white paint without interrupting the flow of the line, massive correcting may destroy the naturalness of the picture.

Materials

Surface
Smooth cartridge paper

Size
6.5in × 9in (16cm × 22cm)

Tools
2B pencil
Dip pen
Medium nib
No 2 sable brush

Colors
Black waterproof India ink
White designer's gouache

Medium
Water

1. With a 2B pencil, roughly sketch in the horse's head and area to be worked within.

2. Develop the eyes with fine crosshatching. If any area of the drawing becomes too dense, it may be corrected with a small sable brush and gouache.

3. Work down the head indicating musculature with a light, diagonal stroke.

4. Block in the surrounding area with broad, dark strokes. To create a darker tone, work back over these strokes in another direction.

5. Put in the darkest areas with a scribbling motion and plenty of ink. Redefine the outlines of the head with a dense, dark line.

6. Work back into the head and surrounding area with crosshatching to create darker tones and shadow areas.

Beginning details · correcting

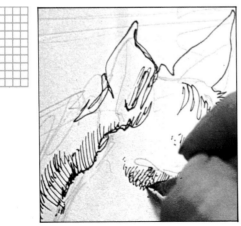

With a very fine
nib, the artist puts in
details around the
eye.

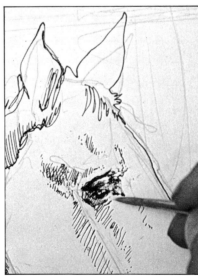

Small areas of ink
can be corrected by
using a small brush
and white designers'
gouache. This can
be used for small
corrections only.

PEN AND INK is considered best suited for tight detail work and densely cross-hatched drawing; however, it is just as possible to use it for loose and informal work. When what are often considered 'mistakes' – such as blending, running, smudging and blotting – are incorporated into the technique, a pen and ink drawing can take on new meaning.

In the drawing here, the artist has taken advantage of all these factors and incorporated them without losing either the strength of the drawing or the subject. Little attempt has been made to control the line of the pen – something many artists struggle hard to achieve – but, instead, the artist has let the nib catch and jump across the page without interference. While working, the artist's eye rarely left the subject; there was a direct line between what was seen and what appeared on the paper, resulting in a series of lines and marks which possibly suggest the subject better than careful and analytical rendering would have.

When the artist's goal is to capture the essence of the subject rather than creating a nice drawing, the attempt to control will hinder rather than help. In which case it is much better to assume an open attitude and allow the hand to follow the eye naturally and without interference.

Materials

Surface
Stretched white cartridge paper

Size
14in × 19.5in (35cm × 49cm)

Tools
No 2 sable brush
Dip pen
Medium nib

Colors
April green
Black
Blue
Red

Medium
Water

Using side of the pen · finishing details

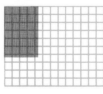

Although a medium nib is being used, a thick line is produced by turning the pen on its side and pulling it across the surface.

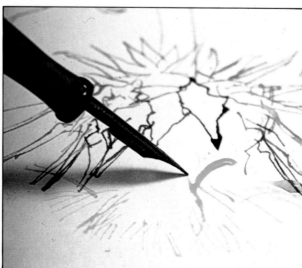

1. To dilute the color, dip the pen in water and then green ink and begin to describe the general outline of the plant. Repeat with red and black inks.

2. Move down the thistle with green ink letting the pen create a rough outline. Do not attempt a careful rendering but let it drag across the paper.

The artist is here describing the final details of the thistle over the light green wash. An irregular, jagged line is achieved by loading the nib with ink and letting it drag across the surface.

3. Dip the pen in water and then blue ink. Begin to put in the flower shape with quick, directional strokes. Dip the pen in black ink and redraw the outline.

4. Continue with the black ink working back over the lines previously drawn in green. Again, do not attempt a smooth line but let the nib catch on the paper.

5. When the drawing is partially dry, mix a light wash of green and water and with a No 2 sable brush quickly block in the general color areas.

6. Dilute blue ink and work into the flower with the same brush. With a clean dry brush and pure undiluted ink, put in the leaf shapes.

Pastel

THE STILL life can be an excellent way for the artist to explore various media and experiment with different ways of seeing. The choice of objects and their arrangement is virtually infinite; the artist can pick and choose and arrange his subject to suit every need.

In this pastel, the artist chose to work with simple objects and a few bold colors. While this may at first seem the easier course to take – as opposed to complex subject matter and color schemes – to work with a few primary colors and a simple subject can often be a very difficult task. The main problem in working with bold colors is how to control their intensities so that one does not overpower the other. Although tones and hues may be altered and adjusted by blending, to retain the freshness and vibrancy of the individual colors demands that the artist carefully balance and weigh individual color areas. One way to ensure a balanced picture is to introduce a complementary color into a general color area. Thus in this picture there are small strokes of red within predominantly blue areas, and vice versa. This will also help to give the picture unity, as the observer's eye will pick up the individual colors as it moves around the picture.

Materials

Surface
Pastel paper

Size
18.5in × 26in (46cm × 65cm)

Tools
HB pencil or willow charcoal
Tissues or rags
Fixative

Colors
Blue-green	Pale blue
Cobalt blue	Pink
Red	Prussian blue
Green	Yellow
Orange	

After the initial areas of color have been laid down, the artist works back over these to strengthen tones.

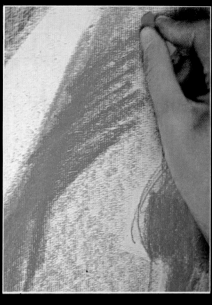

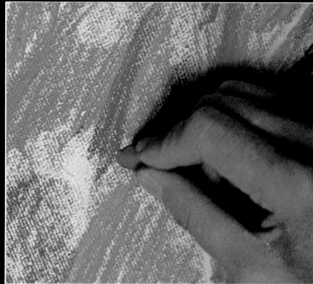

Overlaying thin strokes of pure color will create an optical color mixture on the drawing surface.

1. After lightly sketching the subject in with pencil, use the side of the chalk to put in the main color areas in blue, green, and orange.

2. Using the end of the chalk, begin to work up stronger colors with sharp, directional strokes.

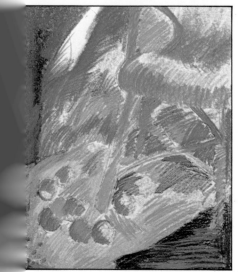

Finished picture · strengthening tones · mixing color · textures

The finished picture shows a skilful handling of strong primary colors to create a balanced and dynamic image. Compositionally, the use of forceful diagonals adds to the overall vitality of the picture.

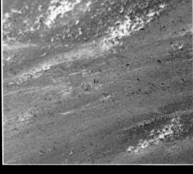

The surface texture is clearly seen in this picture; dense areas of color are mixed with white gaps in the paper to create a gradated effect.

3. Begin to describe lights and darks in green areas by using various tones of green. Carry the red tone into the blue of the backdrop.

4. Intensify dark areas with dark green, Prussian blue, and dark red.

5. With pale blue, work into the foreground area as a highlight and tone down the background with the same color.

ARTISTS WHO experiment with oil pastels quickly grasp their potential for producing strong, brilliant pictures. They are an extremely flexible medium and can be used either like traditional chalk pastels in thin layers of color, or painted on to the surface by softening them with turpentine and applying them with a palette knife.

The picture shown here illustrates the intensity and brilliance characteristic of oil pastels in creating an interesting and dramatic picture. They are best suited to bold, colorful work, although it is just as possible to work with subtle overlays of color. There is a possibility of the surface being built up too quickly, but the artist can always scratch back into the pastel with a sharp tool to either clean up the surface or draw in fine lines of detail.

The composition of this drawing is particularly striking in its use of strong shapes, colors, and the clean white space of the paper. The lack of any additional background information in no way detracts from the forcefulness of the image and, if anything, causes the subject to stand out in bold relief.

Materials

Surface
Rough, heavyweight drawing paper

Size
21in × 23in (52cm × 57.5cm)

Tools
HB pencil

Colors
Black	Medium red
Dark blue	Pink
Green	Yellow

1. Lightly sketch in the subject with an HB pencil.

2. With a medium red pastel, work over the jacket outlines and block in red with light, broad strokes.

3. With dark blue, rough in the shadow areas with light strokes.

4. With a medium yellow, put in the trim on the jacket. With the same red as before, put in the red of the shoes. Do the same with a green pastel.

5. With medium yellow, block in the rest of the shoe color, pressing the pastel hard into the surface.

6. Work back into the jacket with the medium red, bearing hard against the surface. Rework the shadow areas with the same pressure.

7. Continue the previous step until the entire jacket area is covered.

8. Work over the red in the jacket with deep blue, strengthening shadow areas. With a pink pastel, put in highlights in the jacket.

Color areas · developing the picture

The artist begins
by roughing in the
basic color areas
using a light,
sweeping motion.

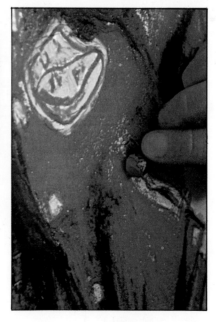

With each
subsequent layer of
color, the pastel is
pressed more firmly
on to the surface to
fill the tiny white
gaps in the paper
grain.

A STILL LIFE need not consist only of the usual subjects such as fruits, glasses and drapery. It is possible to take very ordinary, everyday objects and interpret them in such a way as to create an interesting and stimulating image.

The picture shown here is a good example of the artist taking a subject and, through the use of exaggeration, innovation and careful observation, creating an individual interpretation of a basically commonplace object. The subject was chosen for its lack of color. On first glance, the viewer sees only tones of grey and white; however, on careful observation it becomes apparent that within these general color areas are myriads of subtle colors and tones. Very slight and subtle color variations were discovered within the subject which were emphasized and exaggerated, Thus, where the white of the tiles turns into a coolish blue, the artist described this in much stronger blues and purples; where the tone turns warmer and pinker, a strong orange or red are used.

This method of drawing – exaggerating what is seen – not only helps the artist understand color. It also trains the eye to look for hidden tones and subtle nuances of hue.

Materials

Surface
Blue pastel paper

Size
18.5in × 26in (46cm × 65cm)

Tools
HB pencil
Tissues or rags
Fixative

Colors

Blue-green	Light orange
Cadmium red	Light yellow
Cerulean blue	Orange
Cobalt blue	Pale blue
Light green	Prussian blue

1. After sketching in the subject roughly in pencil, use the side of the pastel to put in broad color areas of white, yellow, and cerulean blue.

2. Blend these areas with a small piece of tissue. With orange, overlay the warmer color areas. With red chalk, draw in the outlines of the tiles in the floor and wall.

3. Using pale blue and light green, begin to develop the cooler, shadow areas in the tiles. Carry red and orange tones over the rest of the picture.

Developing details

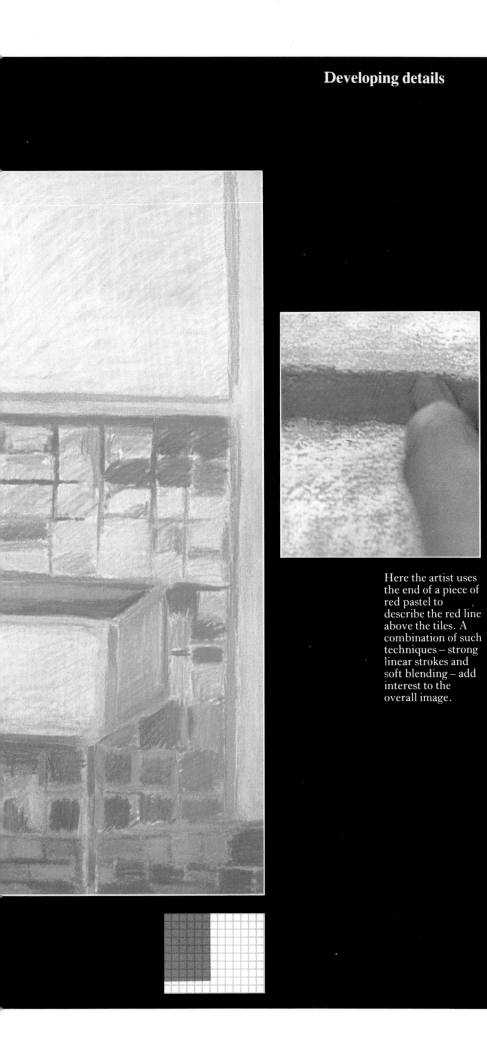

Here the artist uses the end of a piece of red pastel to describe the red line above the tiles. A combination of such techniques – strong linear strokes and soft blending – add interest to the overall image.

4. Lay in red, pink and orange over blue areas to create purplish tones. Begin to put in warm tile colors in yellow and orange.

5. Put in pale green strip on right and in the tiles. Strengthen red and blue strips to the left.

6. Overlay white area above the sink with light orange and yellow and blend with fingers or tissue.

Pencil

A STILL LIFE arrangement can be an excellent vehicle for the study of color, shape, and structure. The still life may take any form from the traditional subject of fruit and flowers to a jumble of objects randomly selected from whatever is at hand. Choose objects which offer an interesting pattern of forms; develop contrasts and harmonies in the range of colors and between geometric and irregular shapes.

The final effect of this drawing is created by successive overlaying of lines in different colors, woven together to create a range of subtle hues. Each layer is described by lightly hatching and crosshatching to gradually build up the overall effect. Blue and purple form rich, deep shadows in the yellows; a light layer of red over yellow warms up the basic color without overpowering its character.

Materials

Surface
Cartridge paper

Size
23in × 23in (57cm × 57cm)

Tools
HB pencil

Colored pencils
Black	Purple
Burnt sienna	Scarlet
Burnt umber	Ultramarine blue
Cobalt blue	Yellow
Grey	Yellow ochre

Finished picture · describing details · overlaying color

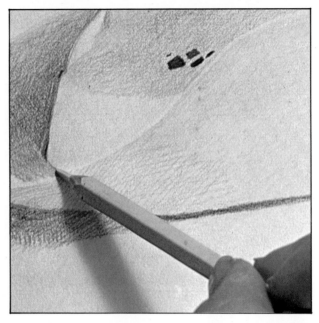

The finished picture (right) illustrates how colored pencil may be used to create a subtle, atmospheric image. The combination of soft tones with a strong composition create a balanced and interesting image.

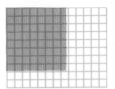

Subtle color tones are created by overlaying light strokes of color. Here the artist works over a shadow area with a light yellow pencil.

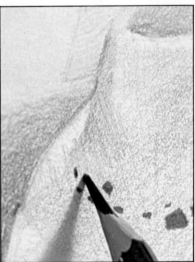

Small detail areas are described with a dark pencil. This is sharpened to a fine point.

1. Lay in a block of light blue shading behind the hat, varying the direction of the pencil strokes. Use the same blue for shadows on and around the hat.

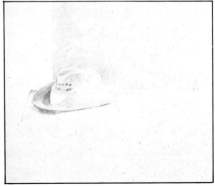

2. Strengthen and broaden the background color. Develop the shadows and pattern details of the hat. Draw in the shape of the boxes with yellow and red pencils.

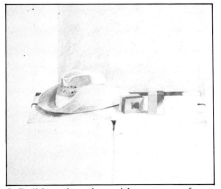

3. Build up the colors with contrasts of tone. Use purple in shadows under the hat, and darken blues to make the objects stand out from the background.

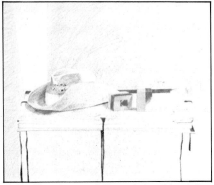

4. Outline the portfolio and sketchbook in black. Strengthen the bright colors against the neutral greys.

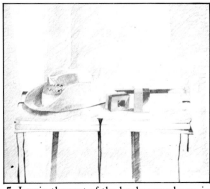

5. Lay in the rest of the background area in blue and vary the tones by heavily reworking. Build up details of line and tone with black and yellow ochre.

MANY OF THE products of graphic designers are the inspiration for still life paintings. There are any number of designs and patterns, bright colors and vivid images, all deliberately designed to be eye-catching, which the artist can exploit to create a stunning painting or drawing.

Any technique which aims to reproduce a detailed surface pattern demands patience and precision. Because the colors used in packaging tend to be intense and artificial, the bright colors of colored pencils are well suited to this type of subject matter.

The colors are solidly blocked in with heavy shading with patterns following curves, angles, and reflections of the objects. These factors all serve to modify the shapes and tones.

Because the image is complex, it is best to draw every detail first with an ordinary pencil. Graphite pencil is more easily erased than colored pencil, so all corrections can be made before the color is applied. Keep the outlines light, and follow them closely when blocking in the color.

Materials

__Surface__
Cartridge paper

__Size__
20in × 24in (50cm × 60cm)

__Tools__
HB pencil
Putty eraser

__Colors__
Black	Purple
Dark green	Scarlet
Emerald green	Yellow
Magenta	Yellow ochre

1. Draw up the still life in outline with an HB pencil. Work on each shape in detail to show the surface designs.

3. Continue to build up the color, working with solid shapes and heavy lines.

5. Gradually extend the color across the drawing. Describe the patterns exactly as they appear on each object.

2. Start to work into one shape in color. Thicken the outline of the lettering with a black pencil and shade in the colored patterns with green and yellow-brown.

4. Work over another shape with thick red, following the pencil outlines precisely and shading in all directions.

6. Draw into each shape in the drawing in turn, developing the color and completing the patterning.

Shadow areas

Using a sharpened pencil, the artist works back into color areas to create darker tones. The shape of the tins is largely created by this gradation of tone.

THIS PICTURE illustrates how willow charcoal, although a fragile medium, can create a very dramatic finished drawing. The drawing process was one of working up dark areas and then modifying them with a putty eraser to achieve a balance between light and shadow. There is a constant movement between the building up of dark areas, lightening them, and then working back into the shadow areas – and then repeating the entire process.

In all drawing media, and particularly with charcoal, it is to your advantage to experiment with the various textures and tones the medium is capable of producing. From a very fine, fluid line to a heavy and dense black, charcoal is flexible enough to fulfil every creative need. Because it is so easily erased, artists feel comfortable with willow charcoal. Where it can be difficult to lay down strong paint colours, with charcoal the artist can let his imagination run free without fear of spoiling a picture, as any mistake is easily corrected or altered.

Materials

Surface
Cartridge paper

Size
20in × 24in (50cm × 60cm)

Tools
Light and medium willow charcoal
Putty eraser
Tissues
Fixative

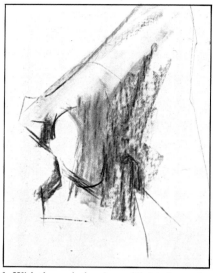

1. With the end of a piece of light charcoal, rough in the general shapes. Using the side of the stick, begin to block in the various shadow areas.

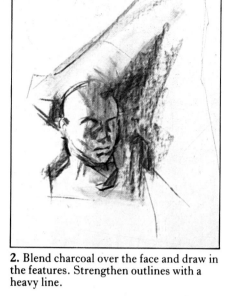

2. Blend charcoal over the face and draw in the features. Strengthen outlines with a heavy line.

3. With a putty eraser, erase out highlight areas in cast and fabric.

4. With medium charcoal, put in shape and shadows in the fabric and the area around the head. Draw in the outline of the fabric and the table.

5. Work back into the head using the side of a piece of light charcoal. Blend with a piece of rag or a finger.

6. Blend the background shadow. With the putty eraser, lighten all shadows by lightly drawing the eraser across the surface.

Finished picture · facial details · using a putty eraser

The attractive qualities of using willow charcoal are shown in the finished picture. By a skilful handling of tone and texture, the artist has produced an unusual still life. Note in particular the combination of different textures and shapes to add visual interest.

Here the artist puts in dark facial details using the tip of the charcoal.

By using a putty eraser, the artist can erase back through the charcoal layer to create highlights and subtle tones of grey.

Pen and ink

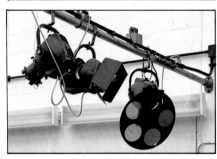

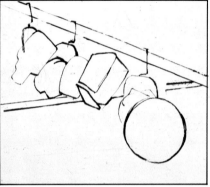

1. Sketch in the outline of the shapes with a pencil to establish the basic positions. Using this drawing as a guide, work with a thick-nibbed pen to define the main shapes.

2. Work boldly in line, drawing into the objects in more detail.

PEN AND INK is a bold, direct drawing medium and therefore demands a degree of confidence in its user. The drawing must be clearly defined through careful observation of the subject and strong interpretation on to the drawing surface. Describe the shapes and contours of each object and use surface detail only where it clarifies and adds texture to the form.

The composition can be sketched out lightly in pencil at the start to establish proportions and relationships of the objects. This should only be a light guideline since the aim is not to trace over the pencil drawing with ink, but to fulfil the medium's potential through direct drawing. Vary the line quality by using thick and thin nibs and so distinguish between solid, hard-edged objects and fine, linear details.

Any initial errors in the drawing can provide a structure on which to more boldly and accurately develop the image. Unwanted marks can be removed by painting over them with a thin layer of white gouache. When this is dry, the shapes can be redrawn in ink. The paint must be applied sparingly as the ink will not work over thick paint and the drawing loses vitality if corrections are too heavy.

Materials

Surface
Thick cartridge paper

Size
25in × 18in (62cm × 45cm)

Tools
Pen holder
Large, square nib
Small mapping pen
No 5 round sable brush

Colors
Black waterproof India ink
White designers' gouache

Medium
Water

With a fine nibbed pen, the artist works back over the initial pen sketch, darkening and broadening outlines.

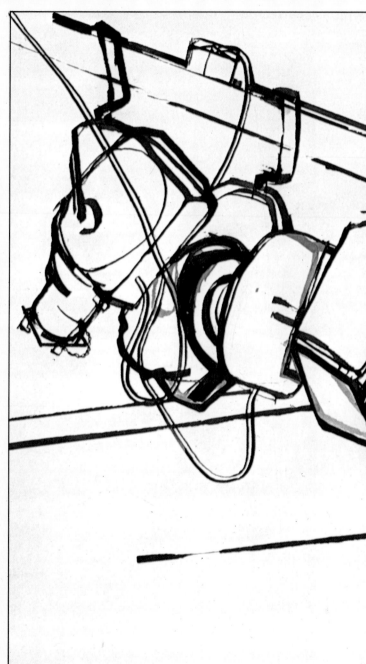

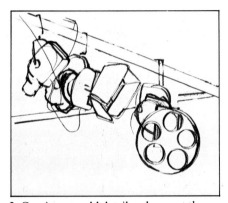

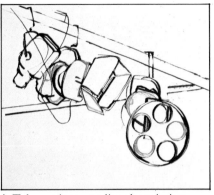

3. Continue to add detail and correct the basic shapes, building up a dense network of lines. Use a fine mapping pen to vary the texture.

4. Take out incorrect lines by painting them over with white gouache. Keep the paint thin so that ink can be applied over it later on during the drawing.

5. Pick out areas of dark tone and pattern with heavy strokes of the broad nib. Keep a balance between plain and patterned areas, thick and fine lines.

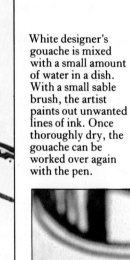

Redefining outlines · using white gouache

White designer's gouache is mixed with a small amount of water in a dish. With a small sable brush, the artist paints out unwanted lines of ink. Once thoroughly dry, the gouache can be worked over again with the pen.

WHILE IT IS possible to describe a subject with accuracy and precision, a picture often needs some creative license to make it more interesting. In this case, the artist has taken the general shape, composition, and color of the subject and through an individual use of line and color washes has exaggerated features to make the picture more descriptive. The techniques used are washed-in color, line, and crosshatching, juxtaposed to create an interesting combination of textures.

One important aspect of this drawing is the use of negative space to define details. In the finished picture, the laces outside of the boot have been created by the use of line. Moving on to the boot's surface, it is the area of colored wash surrounding the white of the paper which continues the image of the lace rather than the pen line itself.

Materials

Surface
Cartridge paper

Size
15in × 22in (38cm × 58cm)

Tools
Pen holder
Small nib
No 2 sable brush
Palette

Ink colors
Black waterproof India ink
Burnt sienna
Red

Medium
Water

1. Begin to put in the outline, varying the line by moving the pen both quickly and slowly. Dip a brush in water and let the pen line bleed into that wet area.

2. Carry the outline further down using red ink. Begin to create shadow textures within the boot with the same red, applied in directional strokes.

3. Mix a small amount of red and burnt sienna and work into the other boot. With pen and black ink, rework the outline of the boot allowing the ink to run.

4. With mixture of red and black ink, crosshatch in the remaining white area of the right boot, leaving parts of the surface untouched to create laces and holes.

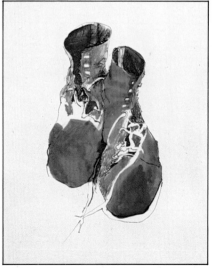

5. Using the pen and black ink, work back into the shoe with crosshatching strokes to create the area around the laces.

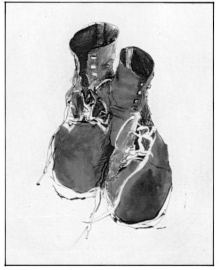

6. Using the back of the pen dipped in the black ink, roughly describe the sole of the boots.

Finished picture · preliminary wash · back of pen · negative space and line

The artists completed the picture by laying a darker wash over shadow areas in the left shoe.

The preliminary wash is put in and will later be worked over with pen and ink.

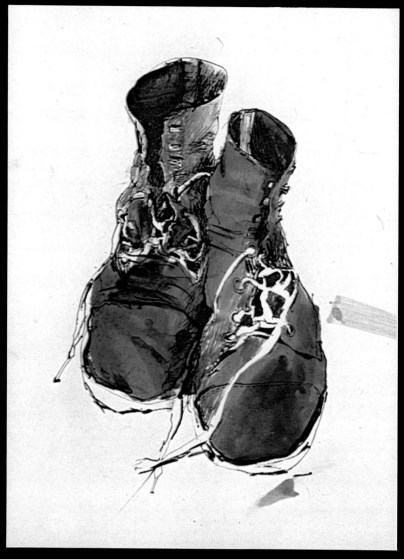

Using negative space to describe shape, the artist uses a hatched tone to create a white area.

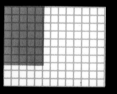

By turning the pen on its back, the artist is able to create a rough, jagged line.

ALTHOUGH THE rapidograph is used largely by the commercial artist, it has gained popularity with the fine artist as well.

As a drawing tool, the instrument has advantages and disadvantages. On the positive side, the artist need not constantly stop to dip the pen in ink, as the reservoir inside the rapidograph provides a constant source. The rapidograph line tends to be more consistent and even than the traditional pen and ink, and less apt to blot. On the negative side, the rapidograph can be finicky and temperamental. The pen must be kept in a near-upright position while drawing and frequently shaken to keep the ink flowing. The line produced is fine and descriptive, but the artist must first acquire a sensitive touch to obtain this effect.

While the drawing illustrated could have been produced with the traditional pen, ink and nib, only a rapidograph could achieve the smooth, consistent line work as seen in the seat of the chair.

The subject was modelled by the use of hatching and crosshatching many fine lines to give the impression of depth and contour. To create deep, dark shadows, the artist put layers of strokes one over the other. Note that where line was used within the coat, it was softened and blurred by the use of crosshatching.

Materials

<u>Surface</u>
Cartridge paper

<u>Size</u>
11in × 14.5in (27cm × 36cm)

<u>Tools</u>
Rapidograph
Medium nib pen
HB pencil

<u>Colors</u>
Black rapidograph ink

1. With an HB pencil, lightly sketch in the subject. Use a rapidograph and black ink to develop shadow tones with hatching and crosshatching.

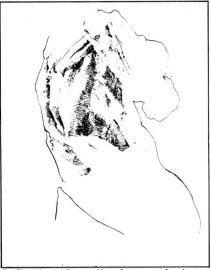

2. Continue the outline downward using a light touch. Work into the line with hatching to create an impression of shadows and folds.

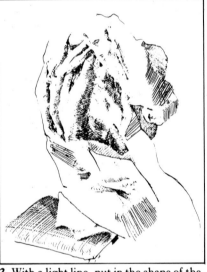

3. With a light line, put in the shape of the chair seat. With light, loose strokes, hatch in tone of the chair seat, crosshatching to create the shadow area.

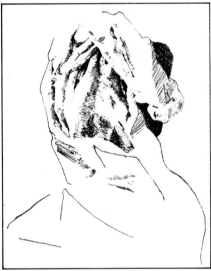

4. Develop darker areas with very fine hatching strokes. Strengthen dark outlines within the shadow areas.

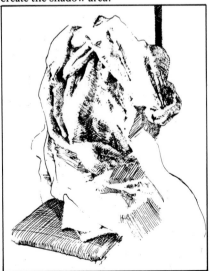

5. Put in the background shadow with broad, diagonal lines, crosshatching lightly to create darker tones.

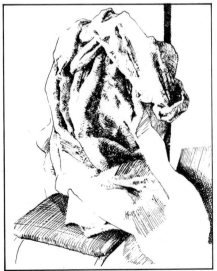

6. Continue to create background shadow area by crosshatching. Vary the direction of the line within these areas.

Creating tone

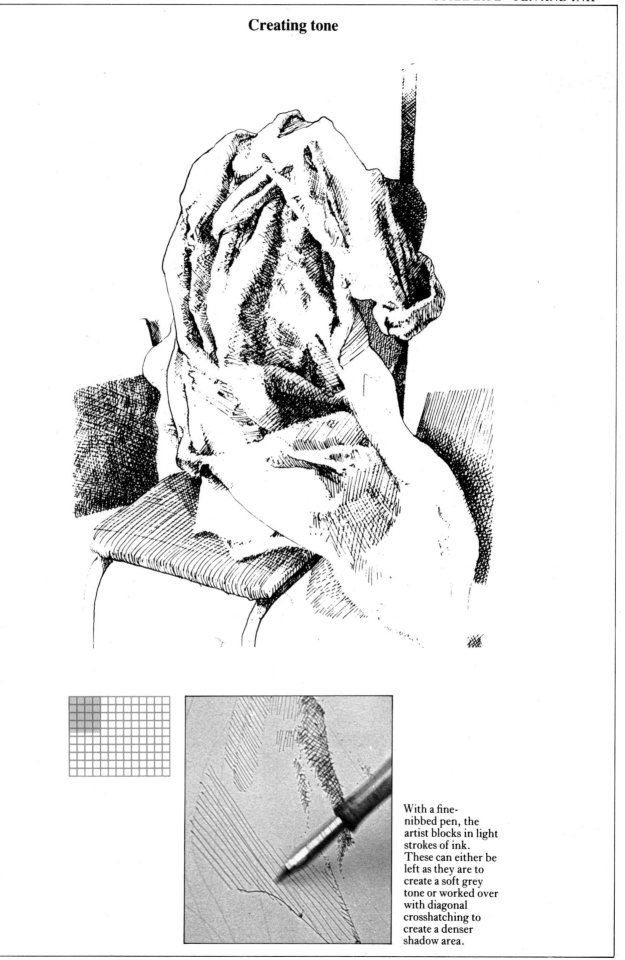

With a fine-nibbed pen, the artist blocks in light strokes of ink. These can either be left as they are to create a soft grey tone or worked over with diagonal crosshatching to create a denser shadow area.

Pastel

PASTEL drawing requires a combination of drawing and painting skills. It can be treated either as a linear medium for outlines and loosely hatched textures, or the color may be laid in broad, grainy patches and blended with the fingers or a rag. Pastel color is soft and powdery and, although it is held together by the tooth of the paper, the surface is always unstable. The drawing should be sprayed with fixative frequently to hold the image while further layers are applied.

The rich textures are built up in a series of overlaid marks, carefully manipulated to describe the forms in terms of their component shapes and color relationships. In this drawing, the pastel strokes have a vertical emphasis, but sometimes marks follow the direction of the forms in order to emphasize a particular curve or angle. It is easier to control the overall image if the strokes follow one direction. In the initial stages of the drawing use medium soft pastels, graduating to the soft type to develop texture as the drawing progresses.

Materials

Surface
Tinted rag paper

Size
23in × 30in (57cm × 75cm)

Tools
Fixative

Colors
Black	Light yellow
Cobalt blue	Olive green
Dark brown	Red
Flesh	Venetian red
Grey	Ultramarine blue

1. Mark the position of the head and limbs with a pink pastel tint and roughly block in the structure of the figure with pink, light yellow, brown and grey.

2. Work lightly over the whole figure, weaving colors together so basic shapes and tones begin to emerge. Use grey and blue to suggest dark tones.

4. Develop cool tones in the drapery with light blue and white and darken the background color with broad vertical strokes of olive green and ultramarine.

5. Work over the composition with tones of grey to strengthen shadows. Draw into the figure with light yellow and dark red to build up the solidity of the form.

7. Intensify the blues in the background, laying in brown and green to vary the color. Develop the colors over the whole drawing, altering if necessary.

8. Emphasize highlights with yellow and white and lighten the background colour with cobalt blue and white. Add touches of warm pink tones into the drapery.

3. Spray the work lightly with fixative. Start to build up a contrast of cool and warm tones using blue and green in the shadow areas.

6. Overlay the colors so that the pastel strokes remain visible but the image works as a whole form. Work over the figure to heighten the tonal contrasts.

9. Round out the forms of the figure using a dark flesh pink, contrasted with cool green in the shadows. Use pinks and browns to warm the drawing.

Finished picture · blocking in · using pure color

As seen in the finished picture, it is the combination of forceful, vertical strokes used to define a largely horizontal subject which creates a harmonious, stable image.

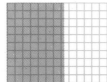

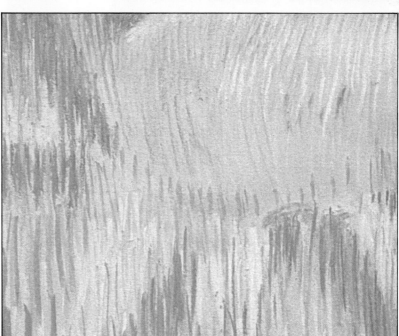

Thin lines of pure color are laid down in directional strokes next to and on top of one another.

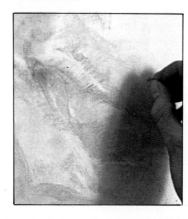

In the first few stages of drawing, the artist describes large areas of color using the side of the chalk.

IN COMMON with watercolor, pastels allow the artist to create layers of transparent colour. These can be used either to subtly imply warm or cool tones or to indicate shadow or highlight areas.

The picture here relies basically on the use of warm and cool tones to create the flesh tones and give the picture unity. The artist worked by developing highlights and shadows, constantly adjusting and readjusting these to correct the balance of warm and cool colors.

Note that pastel cannot be easily erased. If you use a light hand throughout the drawing process, however, you will avoid building up a heavy and unworkable surface.

Compositionally, the drawing was planned to focus attention on the head of the model rather tham the complete torso. By leaving the figure relatively untouched except for a few sparse outlines, and working well into the head and background areas, the artist ensured that the viewer's attention would be focused on the head – the most important area of the picture.

Materials

Surface
Cartridge paper

Size
18.5in × 26in (47cm × 65cm)

Tools
Large soft brush
2B pencil
Putty eraser
Fixative

Colors
Light grey
Dark grey
Black
White

1. Reinforce pencil outlines with pastel. Use a deep tone for the hair and shadow areas of the face.

2. Continue to sketch in the figure in loose outline and block in the background and figure using the same tone.

3. Lighten the background area and carry this tone into the face. With a soft brush blend the background and face.

4. Heighten shadow areas in the face with a deeper tone and work into highlights with a lighter tone.

5. Describe background in more detail and carry this tone into the hair area. Blend the face with a large, soft brush.

6. Using pure white, cover the face area with directional strokes and blend with the brush.

Using pure white · blending with brush

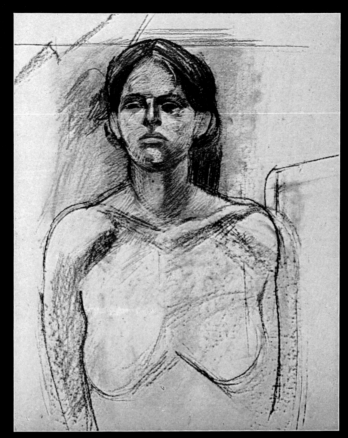

Besides using a rag or fingers to blend, a large, soft sable brush is a useful tool. The artist is here blending strong highlight tones into the darker underlayer.

Using pure white, the artist lays in strong strokes which will be blended and modified by other colors. Note the use of directional strokes to model the face.

Pencil

MUCH LIKE CRAYONS, colored pencils are often overlooked as an exciting drawing medium. As seen in this drawing, they are capable of producing brilliant colors and dramatic tones. The picture is interesting not only for the techniques used in describing the form, but for the unusual and striking composition as well.

In terms of technique, the artist used a combination of heavy, dense shadow areas and lighter, translucent highlights. These play off one another to both heighten and modify the overall effect of the picture. Note that the drawing process is very similar to the traditional oil painting process; thin layers of pure color are laid over one another to build up a shimmering, translucent surface. While it appears that many individual tones and colors have been used, the artist has in fact used only a few warm and cool colors. The flesh tone is used all over the figure and altered for highlight and shadow areas by either overlaying warm red tones for highlights or cool blues for shadows.

Compositionally, the artist has exploited the white of the paper, using it to become part of the drawing as demonstrated in the playing cards and sunglasses. This is extremely effective in creating unity between the image and its environment, as well as strengthening the intensity of colored areas.

Materials

Surface
Cartridge paper

Size
14in 14in (35cm × 35cm)

Tools
Putty eraser

Colors

Black	Pale blue
Blue-violet	Purple
Green	Red
Orange	Yellow

1. Sketch in the figure very lightly with a 2B pencil. With heavy strokes, put in the hair in black and light blue outside of the head. Mix black and red in the glasses.

2. Overlay thin layers of purple and blue in the shoulder areas.

3. Work over the shoulder with a thin layer of orange. Move down the arm and breast, again leaving the paper bare to describe white areas. Carry blue shadow down.

4. With cool blue or purple and overlaying warm flesh tones, put in the right shoulder. Very loosely describe the blue shadow at the right of the head.

5. Varying warm tones of orange, red, and yellow, lightly work down the figure. Continue to use cool blue or purple for shadow areas.

6. Work down over the stomach area with the same warm and cool tones. Keep shadow areas dense and clearly defined.

Finished picture · using white of paper

Colored pencil should not be overlooked as a forceful tool, capable of producing effects equal to any painting medium. The clean, pure color areas contrast well with any tinted or pure white drawing surface.

This detail clearly shows the use of the white paper, rather than color, to create shapes.

FIGURE DRAWING IN pencil is one of the most useful skills for artists to acquire and is usually included in the first projects given in art schools.

Interesting variations can be obtained by placing the figure in strong light and shadow. If the effect of the light is to be the main interest of the drawing, the picture must be treated as a tonal study by taking advantage of the patterns of light and shade across the forms.

Large areas of pencil shading can become either boring or messy, so the tones must be developed gradually and the textures varied to define separate forms. The dense grey background area in this drawing is built up with layers of fine, criss-crossed marks, loosely woven together to create an overall tone. The shading on the figure is more solid and close-knit, and the dark tones are contrasted with the bare white paper representing the fall of the light.

Materials

Surface
Thick cartridge paper

Size
24in × 16in (60cm × 40cm)

Tools
HB and 2B pencils
Putty eraser
Fixative

1. To establish the scale, start by making a brief outline sketch of the figure. Work into the shape of the head, laying in the darkest tones.

2. Strengthen the outline, working down from the head, and block in dark stripes of shadow cutting across the body. Lay a mid-toned grey behind the head.

Describing tone

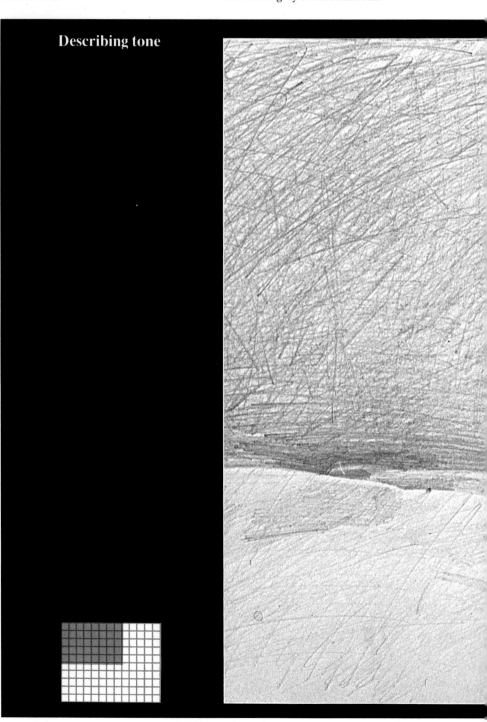

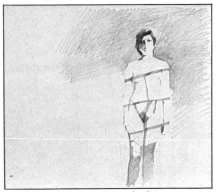

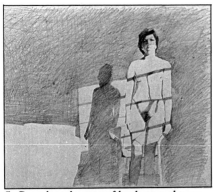

3. Continue to extend the shadow pattern on the figure with dark shading. Develop the background tone, keeping the marks light and loose.

4. Draw into the background behind the figure, lightly outlining shapes with tonal shading.

5. Complete the area of background tone and work back into the shapes of the figure and shadows, building up details in the forms and patterns.

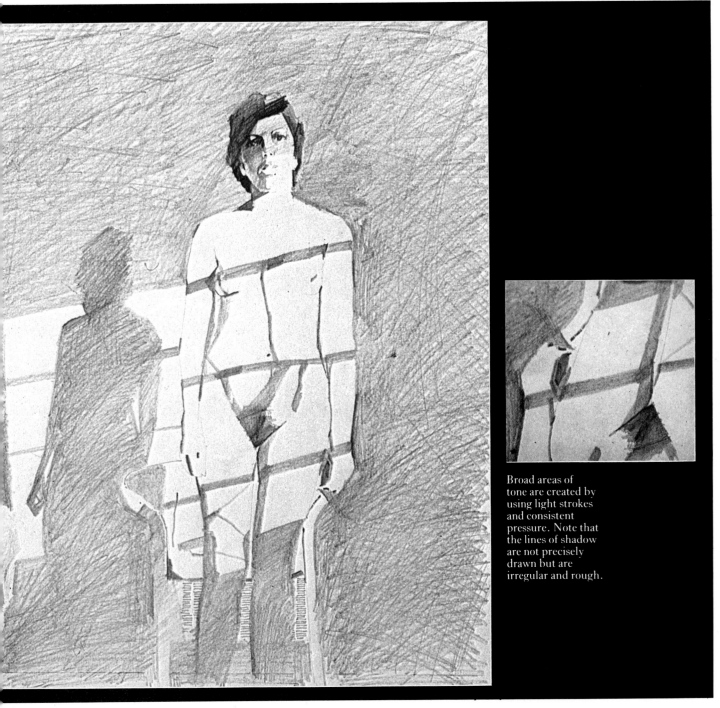

Broad areas of tone are created by using light strokes and consistent pressure. Note that the lines of shadow are not precisely drawn but are irregular and rough.

THE GENERAL impression of this drawing is similar to an old photograph or print due largely to the color of the paper and the soft pencil tones. The picture shows how pencil can be used with a light, subtle touch to create a peaceful, stable atmosphere.

The effect is also similar to the drawings of the French artist Seurat who, by using rough paper and a soft, dark crayon, was able to create tonal areas duplicating the pointillist technique. A rough surface will lessen the linear effect of the pencil and blend tones more evenly than smooth paper.

The artist here depended upon the use of tone to create an illusion of space and depth and, as seen in the head, this can heighten the overall emphasis of the figure within the picture plane. Although most of the page is blank with no indication of the environment, putting the dark shadow area outside the face gives an impression of depth and space.

Materials

Surface
Pumpkin colored pastel paper

Size
16in × 20in (40cm × 50cm)

Tools
2B and 4B pencils
Putty eraser
Tissues
Fixative

1. Lightly sketch in the outlines of the figure with a 2B pencil.

2. Begin very lightly to put in the shadow areas with loose, directional strokes. Add dark details around the neck.

3. Work back into the hair with more pressure, building up darks. Strengthen face and chair outlines.

4. Begin to work outside of the face with very light strokes. Carry this over to the flower shape.

5. Strengthen the shadow areas within the figure. With a 2B pencil, work down the figure, roughing in general outlines and shadow areas.

6. With a 4B pencil, strengthen details of face and flower. With same, darken shadow areas in the dress.

Creating tones with putty eraser

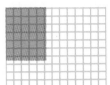

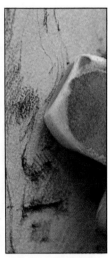

The artist works into the facial details using a combination of grey tones and the clean paper surface to describe shadow and highlight areas.

CHARCOAL IS a most rewarding artistic medium. It gives a characteristic rich, soft black color and a wide variety of textures and tones. However, it is powdery and impermanent, while the drawing may soon become messy and uncontrolled if over elaborated.

Observe the subject carefully as you draw, analysing the shapes and tones, and make your marks decisive and vigorous. Do not attempt to be too precise; a stick of charcoal cannot be as carefully manipulated as the fine point of a pencil, for instance. The best subject is a strong image full of dense tone and calligraphic line. Use a putty eraser both to take out errors and to draw highlights into the loose, black surface. Fix the drawing whenever a stage of the work is successfully completed so that the surface does not become dull and smudgy.

A charcoal drawing on tinted paper can prove particularly effective, especially if white gouache is applied to strengthen the highlights and round out the forms. Use the paint sparingly and keep it free of charcoal dust or it will look dull and grey, deadening the tonal contrasts and producing an opposite effect to the one intended.

Materials

Surface
Tinted drawing paper

Size
16in × 23in (40cm × 57cm)

Tools
No 6 sable round brush
Medium charcoal
Putty eraser
White designers' gouache

Medium
Water

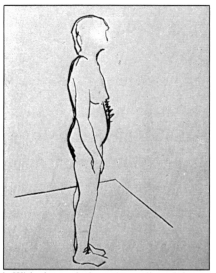

1. With charcoal, draw the outline of the figure with bold, black lines. If necessary, make small corrections or revisions as you work.

2. Start to develop the tonal structure by spreading the charcoal lightly with your fingers and erasing to make grey tones.

3. Lay in broad areas of grey with the side of the charcoal, using the pointed end to draw into the background shapes with loose, calligraphic marks.

4. Block in small areas of solid black around the figure and strengthen the definition of the shapes and patterns with strong lines.

5. Work over the figure adjusting details and strengthening lines. Use the eraser to lighten greys and bring up white highlights.

6. Apply thin patches of white gouache with a No 6 sable brush to add definition to the highlight areas. Let the paint dry before making finishing touches.

Highlighting with gouache

With a small brush and white designer's gouache, strong highlights are developed in the figure. The gouache is allowed to blend with the charcoal to create subtle grey tones.

Highlighting with gouache

THE OVERALL EFFECT of a drawing executed in pure graphite powder is a subtle, impressionistic one, as if the artist had taken a fleeting glance and quickly described the basic tones and shapes of the subject. Graphite is best used for describing tones, not for creating a highly rendered, detailed drawing. When applied with the fingers, the artist can render the figure in contours and directional strokes which both follow and shape the form.

It is this particular aspect – working in tones rather than line – which gives the medium its unique softness and subtlety. However, pure graphite powder has a slippery quality and, because it is so easily applied to the surface, the artist must avoid losing control of the drawing. If mistakes are made however, they can be easily rubbed out with a rag and turpentine.

When used with turpentine, a range of tones can be created from very pale greys to bold and intense blacks. Coupled with the use of a clean pencil line, the tones of the graphite will lend a soft, atmospheric mood, regardless of subject matter.

Materials

Surface
Heavyweight cartridge paper

Size
14in × 18in (35cm × 45cm)

Tools
4B pencil
Putty eraser
Q-tips
Small rags or tissues

Colors
Raw graphite powder
Cerulean blue pastel

Medium
Turpentine

1. Dip fingers in bowl of graphite powder and block in general shadow areas. Rubbing harder will create darker tones.

2. With a 4B pencil, rough in figure outlines and further develop shadows within the figure.

3. Dip a small rag or Q-tip in turpentine and rub on to the surface. Wipe out mistakes or false highlights with a clean rag and turpentine.

4. Dip a clean Q-tip in graphite and work around the figure, darkening the background.

5. Darken the background to bring out light areas. Reinforce figure outlines in pencil. Work around the figure with a rag dipped in turpentine.

Drawing with fingers · blending with turpentine

The fingers are first dipped into the pure graphite powder and then applied directly on to the drawing surface. The pressure and amount of powder will determine the density of tone.

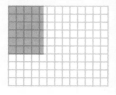

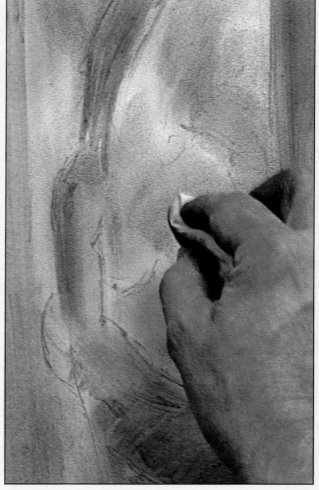

With a small tissue dipped in turpentine, the graphite can be blended and worked to create a variety of tones.

Pen and ink

WHILE PEN AND ink may at first prove uncomfortable and awkward to work with, the artist will soon develop a natural feel for the movement of the pen, the flow of the ink, and which gestures produce which marks. The pen and ink draftsman creates a draw-drawing from the use of the white of the paper, the black of the ink, and the many tones in between these two. These tones are usually created by the use of individual lines of ink which, when laid over one another in various directions, create a mesh-like effect, giving an impression of shadow and depth. Unlike other drawing and painting media, the pen and ink artist is limited to the use of line for developing tone, but, as demonstrated in this drawing, creating a highly modelled, accurate drawing presents no problem despite this limitation.

In this drawing, the artist, with a minimum of detail, has accurately rendered the figure. The simple use of outline and shaded, crosshatched areas alone gives the figure shape, dimension and weight. The tone created by pen and ink can be very subtly varied and need not have a harsh black and white effect, if carefully graduated and controlled. If you look carefully at the area of the hand resting on the knee, you will see that only loose, rough strokes have been used to describe the shadow areas.

Materials

Surface
Smooth cartridge paper

Size
9in × 12in (22cm × 30cm)

Tools
Dip pen
Fine nib
2B pencil

Colors
Black waterproof ink

1. Sketch in the figure very roughly with a 2B pencil. Put in general outlines in ink and begin to describe shadow areas.

2. Continue the outline of the figure and return to put in shadow areas. Use a hatching stroke to define muscles.

3. Continue outline of the arm. Moving outside of the figure, very loosely put in broad strokes, working in one direction.

4. Continue down to hands and legs of figure, putting in outlines and then working into shadow areas with light strokes.

5. Carry background tone down behind the chair using same directional strokes. Leave white of paper bare to define chair shape.

6. Changing the direction of the line, put in general shadow over the leg. Crosshatch over the background shadow to create a denser tone.

Defining shadow areas

Broad areas of
light hatching are
defined by using a
dark outline to
enclose the strokes.

WHILE A large variety of commercial pens and nibs are available, it is interesting to experiment with hand-cut pens made from quills or hollow sticks. A thick reed pen is used here to give a bold, fluid line to create a spontaneous image.

Drawing with line will give the basic outlines of the forms; the image is then given volume by loose washes of thin, wet color. A rich surface texture can be built up with this technique so, although only two colors have been used in this picture, a considerable variety of tonal density is achieved.

The intention is not to depict the subject in meticulous detail, but to record a lively impression of the mood and pose which exploits the freedom and diversity of the medium. If the pen is used on dry paper, or over a dry wash it makes a strong, sharp line. When line is applied into wet layers they will spread and feather. Be careful when drawing into a wet area not to tear the damp paper with the point of the pen. Vary the shapes and tones of the washes to provide a contrast between hard-edged shapes and subtly blended tones so that the full versatility of the medium contributes to the overall effect.

Materials

__Surface__
Stretched cartridge paper

__Size__
18in × 22in (45cm × 55cm)

__Tools__
Hollow piece of reed or willow
Knife or scalpel
No 8 round sable brush

__Colors__
Brown ink
Black waterproof India ink

__Medium__
Water

1. Dip the pen in black ink diluted with water and draw the profile of the head. Using a small sable brush, apply thin washes of brown ink.

2. Continue to build up the washes, preserving areas of white. Use the pen to define the linear shapes in the foreground and background.

Making the reed pen · the pen line

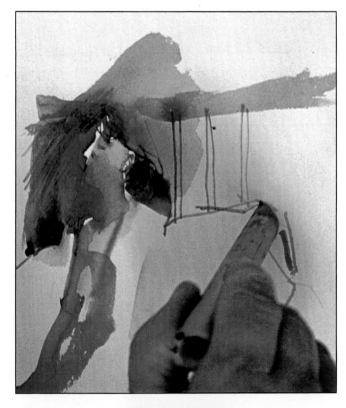

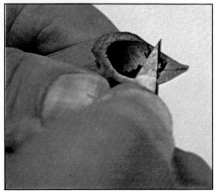

A reed pen can be made from any type of hollow wood. Once roughly shaped, the point is refined with a small knife. The line created by a reed pen is irregular yet soft and produces an effect very suitable for figure work.

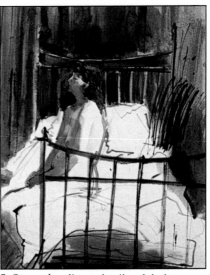

3. Lay in broad washes of diluted brown and black inks, working across the entire picture.

4. Draw the figure in more detail using bold, fluid lines. Enrich the shadows with additional washes of brown and black ink.

5. Strengthen linear detail and dark tones with the pen and brush in black.

A rapidograph was used for this drawing rather than the traditional pen, nib, and ink as it gives a more consistent line. Thus the artist could develop fine areas of crosshatching without fear of dripping. By leaving the white paper untouched for highlight areas and using hatching and crosshatching to describe shadow areas, the artist has created an interesting drawing.

The rapidograph is a sensitive and temperamental tool. The artist must have a light touch and hold the pen nearly upright to keep the ink flowing. The pen should be shaken frequently in this position to make sure the nib does not clog. The paper used with a rapidograph should have a very smooth surface, otherwise the fine hairs of the paper will rip and clog the nib.

Until familiar with the rapidograph, it is worthwhile to experiment with the various textural effects available. Note that in this drawing the artist has used small areas of crosshatching to build up the shadow area, changing the direction of the line to avoid building it up too densely. A huge variety of textures can be created by simply varying the direction and thickness of the line.

Materials

Surface
Cartridge paper

Size
12in × 23in (30cm × 57.5cm)

Tools
Rapidograph
02 nib

Colors
Black rapidograph ink

1. Carry the outline down the figure with the same consistent pressure.

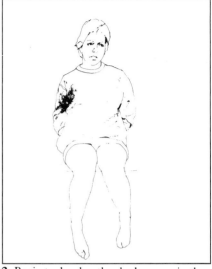

2. Begin to develop the shadow area in the elbow by lightly hatching and crosshatching in small areas, working the line in different directions.

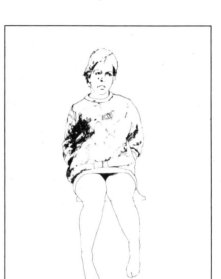

3. Work over the figure and hair developing shadow areas. Watch the balance of light and dark carefully and move back to judge tones.

4. Put in dark areas of the chair seat with dense crosshatching.

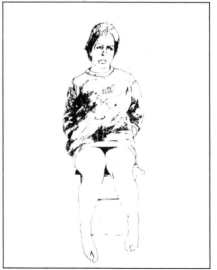

5. Work into the face, and with a very light stroke, put in the shadow areas.

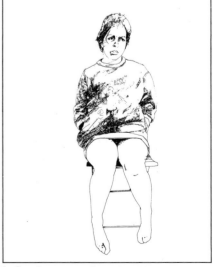

6. Continue to work on the shirt and head, heightening dark areas by overlaying strokes in different directions.

Crosshatching to create tone

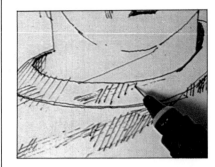

Whether a rapidograph or traditional dip type, the pen relies on the use of line to create tone and texture. Here the use of fine lines of hatching and crosshatching are being used to create subtle tones and shadow areas.

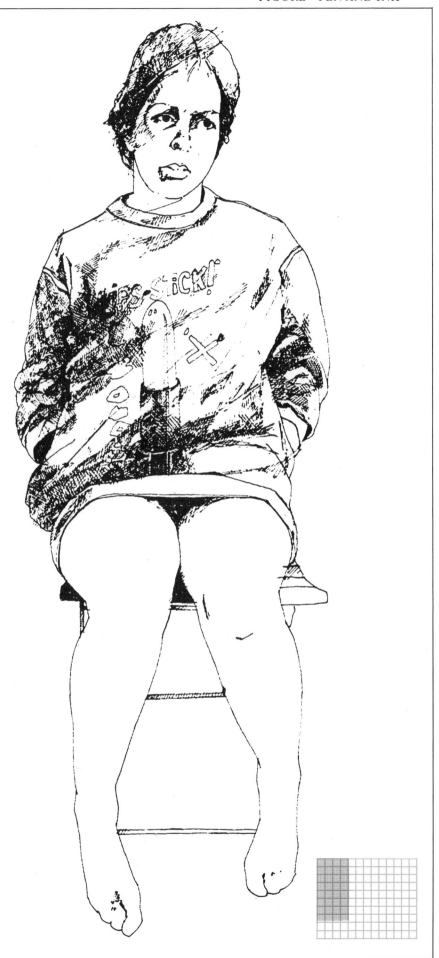

Pencil

TO CREATE a quick, informal portrait, any artist needs to be familiar with the chosen medium and techniques. Naturally, a sound knowledge of human anatomy is beneficial for all figure and portrait artists. Regardless of a person's distinguishing features, what lies beneath the surface – muscles, tendons, bones and cartilage – are the building blocks for all portrait and figure work. If the artist knows, for example, why an eye looks like it does – where it bulges and where it recedes – he will be that much closer to creating an accurate likeness.

This is especially true when doing a quick sketch, as the goal is to capture only the essential and outstanding characteristics of the model as quickly as possible. A labored and detailed drawing would allow the artist to study, correct, and change the drawing; but a quick sketch demands that the artist be able to accurately render the subject, since he will not be able to correct and revise.

Note, for example, how the artist has created the nose of the model and used directional lines to give form and depth. Through constant observation, studying and practice, the artist is able to quickly and effectively capture a likeness of the model.

Materials

Surface
Smooth, heavy weight drawing paper

Size
24in × 30in (60cm × 75cm)

Tools
2B and 4B drawing pencils
Eraser
Tissues or torchon
Fixative

1. With a 2B pencil, sketch in the general shape of the head. Position features in relation to one another, using very light strokes.

3. To bring the nose forward, crosshatch in shadow areas. Develop structure of face with light, widely spaced strokes. Refer to the subject to check the drawing.

5. Draw in the neck and shirt collar. Darken all detailed areas with contour strokes.

2. Begin to work into the shadow areas around the eyes with light crosshatching. Develop the hair with strokes which follow general contours.

4. With a 4B pencil, rework the shadow areas to darken tone. Work back into shadow areas with a putty eraser to erase highlights or lighten tones.

6. Blend in shadow area in neck with tissue or torchon. Put in shadow area outside of the face and blend. Erase back into highlights within the face.

Final details and crosshatching tones

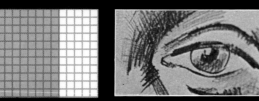

Detailed areas of the drawing are developed in the final stages. Note the use of strokes to develop strong shadow areas.

THIS PICTURE is a good example of the effective use of colored pencils in portraiture, especially when combined with the color of the clean white surface.

Although the artist has used line to develop tonal areas, the method of drawing is similar to the classic oil painting technique of laying down colors one over another to 'mix' new colors. This requires a confident use of color, as once put down, colored pencils are not easily erased. This, combined with subtle or strongly directed strokes which follow or exaggerate the planes of the figure, creates a powerful image.

An interesting feature of the composition is the use of the white paper within the figure to describe the face, hands, and hair highlights. In the model's left hand, one simple line is all that is needed to separate the figure from its environment. The nearly bare areas of the face and hands are heightened by the surrounding dark area, which, in turn, plays off against the white of the paper.

Materials

Surface
White drawing paper

Size
12in × 16in (30cm × 40cm)

Colors
Dark red	Raw umber
Light green	Ultramarine blue
Magenta	Yellow ochre

Initial color areas · dark details

In the final stages of drawing, the artist reworks dark detail areas with a strong blue pencil.

The outlines of the figure are first sketched in with a warm brown. The artist then blocks in shadow areas with a cool blue. Here he is working back into the face with light strokes of orange to begin to build up flesh tones. Note the use of loose strokes.

1. Sketch in the outline of the face in raw umber. Use ultramarine blue for shadows and hair and very light strokes of the same color in the blouse.

3. With red and yellow, put in loose strokes to define hair tone. Strengthen outlines of face with ultramarine blue. Put in dark shadow area to right of face

5. Overlay magenta area with red. Create stronger shadow areas with ultramarine blue.

2. With pale green, begin to define shadow areas of the face with very light hatching and crosshatching. With dark blue, put in the eye details.

4. Work into the hair with directional strokes of red. Overlay light strokes of blue and red in the blouse with loose, scratching strokes.

6. Work back into hair with burnt umber. Use pale green to put in highlights in the cup.

THIS DRAWING RELIES largely on the use of loose, flowing lines and areas of tone to create the image. The drawing was executed rapidly with just essential shapes and tones used to describe the sitter. The emphasis of the drawing is on the face and hands, making the figure a self-contained, stable unit.

A high contrast is developed in the face of the model which, with the use of the pure white paper and very dark details, focuses the viewer's attention on the head area. The relaxed line work and shading within the torso lend the figure both weight and movement. While solid and stable, the impression is that the figure could get up or change his position at any moment. The value of using a quick, informal approach to drawings of this type becomes evident especially when the pose is difficult or uncomfortable for the model and he or she is apt to move or tire easily.

Materials

Surface
Smooth white drawing paper

Size
15in × 16.5in (37.5cm × 41cm)

Tools
2B and 4B drawing pencils
Putty eraser
Fixative
Tissues

1. Sketch in the outlines of the figure very loosely with a 2B pencil. Rough in the eyes, nose, and mouth.

2. With quick, light, directional strokes, put the shadow areas of the hair and figure into the drawing.

3. Work back into the head of the figure with a 4B pencil strengthening dark areas. With the same, outline shoulder and neck.

4. With a 2B pencil work back into the shadow areas. Redefine leg and feet outlines as necessary.

5. With the 4B pencil, go over the lower half of torso with quick, light strokes building up shadow tones. Work back into the head to heighten darks.

6. With the 2B pencil, define fingers and hands. Put in shadow area beneath them.

Using tone and stroke to develop the figure

The shadow areas on the face are developed with diagonal strokes of soft grey tone. Both the tone of the pencil and the direction of the strokes help give the impression of depth and form.

Pastel

THERE IS A long history of pastel portrait drawing and some of these drawings, with their finished surface of subtly blended color, are nearly indistinguishable from an oil painting. In fact, the term 'pastel painting' has become as common as 'pastel drawing'. While the early pastellists most likely spent as much time on their work as a painter would on an elaborate portrait, contemporary artists have developed techniques of drawing which are flexible and less time-consuming than these early drawing methods.

The basic structure of this drawing is built upon woven lines and hatched blocks of tone using a limited range of colour. Once the fundamental shapes and tones are established, the subject is rendered with layers of bright color.

Pastel is powdery and difficult to work with if the surface becomes too densely covered. Thus, it is worthwhile to spray the drawing with fixative frequently to keep the color fresh and stable.

Materials

Surface
Beige pastel paper

Size
25in × 18in (62.5cm × 45cm)

Tools
Soft, large brush for blending
Pastles
Putty eraser
Fixative

Colors
Apple green	Scarlet
Black	Ultramarine blue
Light blue	Venetian red
Pink	White
Prussian blue	Yellow

1. Draw up the basic shapes of the image in Prussian blue, sketching in rough outlines and a brief indication of tones.

3. Refine details of the features with strong lines of dark blue and flesh out the face with solid blocks of white and red.

5. Block in light tones in the face with pink and pale blue. Lay in broad areas of dark tone with black and Prussian blue, working out from the figure.

7. Lay in dark background tones to emphasize the form of the figure. Overlay and blend the colors to mix the tones, working over the whole image.

2. Build up the linear and tonal structure with Venetian red, developing the loose modelling of the forms. Strengthen the drawing with fine black lines.

4. Spray the work with fixative and let it dry. Draw into the figure with blue and black correcting the outlines and adding extra details in line and tone.

6. Develop the intensity of color, using strong, bright hues to lift the overall tone. Link vivid yellow highlights on the face with the same color in the background.

8. Bring out the form with strong white highlights. Apply the pastel thickly and blend the color softly with a dry brush. Strengthen light tones in the background.

Strengthening background and face with black

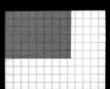

Once general shadow and highlight areas have been blocked in, the artist works back into the picture with a black pastel to develop facial details. Here he is outlining the shape of the glasses.

With a black pastel, the artist darkens the shadow area beside the face. This has the effect of forcing the flesh tones of the face to stand out in bold relief.

THERE ARE good reasons for the fact that many pastel artists prefer to work on tinted paper. In this case, the flesh-toned paper has been used as part of the figure. As well as being a solid, neutral tone, it works to emphasize the strong colours used in the face and dress.

A minimum of blending has been used thus the technique of overlaying colors may be clearly seen. The hands reveal how the artist has used directional strokes of pure color to give them form and tone; throughout the figure the artist has changed the direction of the strokes to describe planes within the face and hands.

Materials

<u>Surface</u>
Pumpkin coloured pastel paper

<u>Size</u>
22in × 30in (55cm × 75cm)

<u>Tools</u>
Tissues or rags
Large, soft brush for blending
Fixative

<u>Colors</u>
Light grey
Dark grey
Black
White

1. Roughly describe the dark areas of the head and torso with loose strokes.

2. Put in hair highlights and eye details. With white, put in strong face highlights and strengthen outlines.

3. Fill in hair area describing shadow and highlights. Rough in chair and flower and draw in the hands.

4. Develop the shadow areas of the hands. If a part of the drawing proves difficult, use the rest of the page to do a detailed study.

5. Block in the lighter area of the chair. Work into shadow areas and blend and lay in the shadow areas in the dress.

6. Roughly describe the dress pattern with a mixture of tones.

Overlaying light tones · doing a detailed study

Here the artist overlays very dark shadow areas in the hair with a lighter, softer shade of brown.

If a part of the drawing proves difficult, a study can be done elsewhere on the page which can later be cropped from the finished picture.

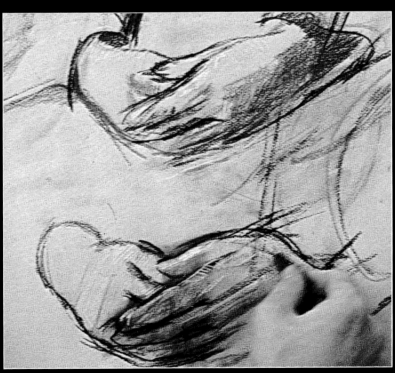

IN CAPTURING THE character of a subject, a quick sketch is often more successful than a carefully worked painting. The loose, vibrant colors of pastels are particularly suited for quick sketches using a vigorous, calligraphic style, as shape and texture can be shown through the activity of the color rather than the meticulous delineation of forms.

In this drawing, pastel strokes are multidirectional and the colors warm and bright, giving an impression of a fleeting image; the model is frozen in a split second of time, not carefully posed for a long sitting. This is a quality which photographers often capture, and thus photographs are often a good source of reference material for this type of portrait.

Tonal contrasts are skillfully manipulated with black used sparingly for dark tones and outlines. Facial shadows are created with mauve and a vivid dark red, and thick white highlights give an impression of light across the face. The movement and texture of the hair is represented by heavily scribbled strokes of bright orange.

Materials

Surface
Blue-grey pastel paper

Size
11in × 15in (27.5cm × 37.5cm)

Tools
Fixative

Colors
Black	Pink
Burnt sienna	Ultramarine blue
Mauve	White
Orange	Yellow

Blending preliminary tones · highlighting the face

After the outlines of the head are sketched in, the artist lays in very thin strokes of warm and cool tones, blending them with his fingers.

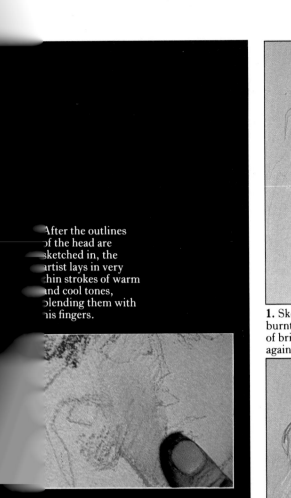

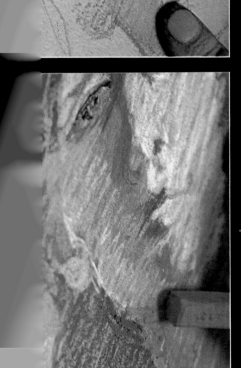

Highlighting the face with strong warm tones. Note how the artist has used strokes of pure color in the shadow areas and how the warm oranges and pinks mix with the cool, tinted paper.

1. Sketch in the outline of the figure in burnt sienna. Work into the face with lines of bright orange, ultramarine and pink against dark shadows in the hair.

2. Hatch in light tones down one side of the figure with broad, grainy strokes of white. Move across the whole figure putting in orange, yellow and blue.

3. Accentuate the shapes in the face with fine black lines and patches of strong colour. Heighten light tones with pink and mauve against warm dark red shadows.

4. Build up the light colour in the face and work over the hair with heavy strokes of black, white and orange.

5. Outline the hand and arm with black and block in dark flesh tones with orange and mauve. Lay in a dark blue background tone.

6. Draw vigorously into all the shapes with strong color, developing the tones and texture and highlighting the face and hand.

Pen and ink

A PROFILE CAN be as successful in capturing a person's likeness as the traditional full-faced portrait because it clearly shows the contours of the individual's features. In this painting, the structure of the form is broken into a pattern of shapes by extremes of light and shadow. A strong image is constructed by using the basic techniques of hatching and stippling. The drawing uses high tonal contrasts, but note that there are no solid black areas; the darkest tones consist of layers of dense crosshatching built up in patterns of parallel lines. Details of texture and shadow in the face are stippled with the point of the nib. The vigorous activity in the drawing is offset by broad patches of plain white paper indicating the fall of light over the form.

Observe the subject carefully as you work, moving the pen swiftly over the paper. Pen strokes should be loose and lively or the result can all too easily look stiff and studied.

Materials

Surface
White cartridge paper

Size
10in × 11.5in (25cm × 29cm)

Tools
HB pencil
Dip pen with medium nib

Colors
Black waterproof India ink

1. Hatch in a dark tone down one side of the head to throw the profile into relief. Continue to build up detail in the face.

2. Work on shadows inside the shape of the head with fine parallel lines slanted across the paper. Work outwards into the background in the same way.

3. Broaden out the shadows and crosshatch areas of the background behind the head to darken the tones.

4. Vary the tones in the background gradually covering more of the paper. Work into the head and clothes with small, detailed patterns.

5. Draw in patches of dark tone to show folds in the clothing. Define the hairline and shape of the ear with crosshatching.

6. Work over the whole image intensifying the tones with hatching and stippling. Develop a high contrast of light and dark down the face and body.

Using paper to model the face

The initial pencil sketch of the head is used only as a reference for developing shadow and highlight areas. Note in particular how the shadows within the face and in the background create the profile of the head.